THE STORY OF MEXICO

Ancient Mexico

THE STORY OF MEXICO

Ancient Mexico

R. CONRAD STEIN

Greensboro, North Carolina

The Story of Mexico: Ancient Mexico
Copyright © 2012 by R. Conrad Stein

Library of Congress Cataloging-in-Publication Data

Stein, R. Conrad.
 The story of Mexico : ancient Mexico / by R. Conrad Stein.
    p. cm.
 Includes bibliographical references.
 ISBN 978-1-59935-161-2
 1. Mexico--History--To 1519--Juvenile literature. 2. Indians of
Mexico--History--Juvenile literature. I. Title.
 F1219.7.S74 2012
 972'.01--dc22

                                         2010041379

Printed in the United States of America
First Edition

Book Cover and interior designed by:
Ed Morgan, navyblue design studio
Greensboro, N.C.

For my wife, Deborah, and daughter, Janna

THE STORY OF MEXICO

Mexican-American War

The Mexican War of Independence

Cortes and the Spanish Conquest

The Mexican Revolution

Benito Juarez and the
   French Intervention

Ancient Mexico

Modern Mexico

Emiliano Zapata and the
   Mexican Revolution

TABLE OF CONTENTS

1 The Land and Its First Inhabitants 9

2 The Olmecs 25

3 The Mystery People and Their Mystery City 37

4 Time and the Maya 53

5 The People of Monte Albán 67

6 Mexico in the Classic Period 77

7 The Toltecs: Warrior/Poets 85

8 The Rise of the Aztecs 95

9 The Feathered Serpent Returns 113

10 The Legacy of Ancient Mexico 129

TIMELINE 133

SOURCES 136

BIBLIOGRAPHY 138

WEB SITES 139

INDEX 140

Warrior of Ancient Mexico, an engraving from
L'Encyclopedie Des Voyages (*The Encyclopedia of Journeys*)
by Jacques Grasset de St. Sauveur, circa 1796

CHAPTER 1

The Land and Its First Inhabitants

It was frosty and probably the winds howled, but still a hardy group of fifteen to twenty men and women pressed forward onto the American continent. They were hunting people and ahead lie their prey— deer, elk, even the giant mammoth. The new land they saw about them posed many dangers, yet it was green, rich, and inviting. Their journey was an unrecorded but incredible event in history. These nameless individuals were the first to enter what was later called the New World.

Today, scholars call the first Americans the Paleo-Indians (*Paleo* from a Greek word meaning "old," and *Indian* after the mistake Christopher Columbus made when he called the Native Americans he encountered "Indians"). How, when, and from where the Paleo-Indians came is a matter of lively and ever-changing debate.

Modern human beings emerged in Africa 100,000 to 200,000 years ago, and they spread to Europe and Asia. An earlier human-like species, the Neanderthal, died out about 35,000 years ago. No Neanderthal remains have ever been found in the Western Hemisphere. Near or perhaps even before the time of the Neanderthal demise, men and women came to the Americas. Those early people were not cave-man types who walked slouched over, carried clubs, and had limited sensitivities. The first Americans were homo sapiens, similar to us in terms of intelligence and ability.

The origin of the migrants or the route they followed is a mystery. The Bering Strait, between Siberia and Alaska, remains a likely path. At the time, the Ice Age gripped the earth and 30 percent of the world's surface was covered with glaciers. With so much water concentrated in ice fields, sea levels were considerably lower than they are in the modern era. Because of the lower sea levels, the Bering Strait—now a string of islands—poked out of the waters to form a continuous land bridge. As a result, the strait presented an inviting avenue.

But the Bering Strait hypothesis assumes that all Paleo-Indians came from Asia. Recent evidence suggests that in the distant past some men and women might have traveled from Europe to the American continent. Groups of European migrants could have taken small boats and sailed along the fringes of the ice fields that once covered the northern regions of the earth. Animals, fish, and birds congregated on the icy shores, providing good hunting for the European travelers.

Historians are also divided as to when the Paleo-Indians arrived. Some say men and women came upon the American continent 35,000 years ago, while others claim 15,000 years is a more accurate estimate. It seems that every new archaeological find sends the actual—provable—arrival date deeper into the past. Given time, Paleo-Indians settled in every habitable part of what Europeans came to call the New World. Within 1,000 years of their first step on North American soil, the ancient people spread from Alaska to Tierra del Fuego at the tip of South America.

Clovis Point Spears

A special spear point that has been found in Mexico and the United States has added to the theory that some Paleo-Indians could have come from Europe. The stone spear tips were named after the town of Clovis, New Mexico, where examples were first found in 1929. They are razor-sharp with a groove partway up their center. The points, which are thought to be more than 13,000 years old, are difficult to carve. Probably each tribe of Paleo-Indians had one or two specialists who acquired the skills to make the spear tips. Interestingly, no such unique points have been found in Siberia, once believed to be the homeland of all Native Americans. But many Clovis-type spear tips have been uncovered in Northern Europe.

Ancient Clovis spear points

Myths and Theories

Myths told by Native Americans in the United States and in Mexico claim their ancestors were created on American grounds, and that they were made there by the gods. Other stories, which scholars denounce as wild speculation, say that early Americans came from the lost continent of Atlantis. Tales also suggest that the first Americans migrated from the Nile Valley in Egypt, bringing with them the knowledge of pyramid-building.

Some 10,000 years ago, Paleo-Indians from the north arrived on the land we now know as Mexico. Again, many reports say that people came to Mexico thousands of years earlier. The first Mexicans were hunters who stalked buffalo, deer, rabbits, squirrels, and birds. They also pursued huge animals that are now extinct—mammoths, mastodons, and a giant bison that was four times the size of the modern species.

Mexico is a long, funnel-shaped country with mountain ranges hugging its two seacoasts. The ranges are the Sierra Madre Occidental on the west and the Sierra Madre Oriental to the east. Between the two mountain ranges lies the broad, relatively flat Central Plateau. Far to the south, at the narrow end of the funnel, the mountain chains come together and the land juts into the Atlantic Ocean to form the Yucatan Peninsula. The word *flat* must be used with caution when describing any aspect of the Mexican landscape. Even the Central Plateau features hills, small mountains, and deep valleys.

A topological map labeling the most prominent mountain ranges in Mexico

Cortés Describes Mountainous Mexico

Hernán Cortés discovered and conquered Mexico for Spain in the 1520s. He was later called before his king, who asked him to describe the new land. According to an often-told story, Cortés fumbled for words while the king sat on his throne growing impatient for an answer. Finally, Cortés picked up a piece of paper from a scribe's table. He crushed the paper into a ball, lay it on a table, tapped it twice with his hand, and said words to the effect, "There, Majesty, Mexico looks like that." It was the only way Cortés could describe Mexico and its endless mountains.

The first Mexicans found a land that was greener, wetter, and far richer in terms of plants and animals than it is today. Tall forests of pine, oak, and fir trees stood on the Central Plateau and in the mountain ranges. Freshwater lakes sparkled in regions that are now deserts. Great flocks of birds flew above the lakes, and the waters teemed with fish. Ancient people gathered at the lakes because they provided water and because it was easier to hunt on the soggy grounds of the lakeshores. Mastodons and other game animals sank in the mud, easing the task of hunters armed with spears.

The Atlatl

Hunters were aided by a spear-throwing device called the *atlatl* (an ancient Mexican word for spear-thrower). An atlatl has a shaft and a cup that is placed at the end of a spear to give the thrower far more leverage. Tests conducted at the Smithsonian Institution demonstrated that, aided by an atlatl, a thrower can hurl a spear the length of a football field and the spear will reach speeds of nearly one hundred miles per hour.

Life was brutal and short for the Paleo-Indians. They traveled in bands of twenty to fifty people, most of whom were related by blood. A man or woman who reached the age of thirty-five was considered a tribal elder. Infant mortality was a grim fact of existence, as the majority of babies died before they reached the age of one year. Still, the ancient Mexicans probably sang songs when they celebrated a successful hunt. Musical instruments such as drums and flutes were played in tribal circles. The Paleo-Indians of Mexico buried their dead, often putting trinkets in gravesites.

Few people lived in prehistoric Mexico or in the Americas as a whole. Dr. Michael D. Coe, a leading expert on Mexico before written history, wrote, "In all the New World prior to 7000 BCE there may never have been at any one moment in time more than a half million persons, with about 30,000 of these in Mexico—a crude guess, to be sure, but not unreasonable."

It is unknown how the isolated tribes greeted strangers. But, based on the behavior of other hunting cultures, it can be assumed that warfare was frequent. Tribes raided neighboring tribes for food. Groups fought for territorial rights to the best hunting grounds. Ancient Mexico was a male-dominated society, as men handled the hunting duties. In almost all prehistoric Mexican languages, the word for "male" was the same as the word for "warrior."

The Ice Age gradually ended, bringing hotter, dryer conditions to Mexico and North America. Climate change killed off grasslands and caused lakes to evaporate. Deprived of food, the huge mammoths and mastodons became extinct. Hunters in ancient Mexico shifted their efforts to smaller animals.

An 1897 painting of a herd of mastadons by Charles R. Knight

They even caught and ate mice. Archeologists have discovered bones of mice that bear the telltale marks of human teeth or knives that scraped off meat. Trees vanished in what is today northern Mexico, and desert conditions prevailed there.

Melting ice caused sea levels to rise. Ocean waters covered much of the Bering Strait, and the ice fields retreated toward the North Pole. The American continent was again isolated from the rest of the world, and many archaeologists believe that immigration to the Americas dwindled or stopped completely for long periods.

Eventually, Mexico developed the climate we know today: a mostly warm and pleasant land where sunshine is almost constant and snowfall is rare. The seacoast regions were hot and humid. Today, the coastal areas of Mexico are called the *tierras calientes* (hot lands). In contrast, the thin air of the mountains and Central Plateau leaves those areas comfortable most of the year. The mountainous regions are known as the *tierras frias* (cold lands), even though they are not at all cold. Rain is unevenly distributed in the country. Along the coasts, rainfall is usually ample. In fact, flooding is often a problem in the *tierras calientes*. However, a frustrating lack of rain plagues the mountains and the Central Plateau.

Rain is seasonal in the highlands. The rainy season begins in June and ends in October. If there was little or no rain during those four months, the Mexicans of old faced hunger. Even today, farmers in the Central Plateau—home to the country's most fertile soil—depend on the rainy season to produce bountiful crops. All the cultures of ancient Mexico worshiped many gods. In the mountainous areas, the rain god was the most important deity in the people's pantheon.

Natural forces presented a host of hazards to the Mexican Paleo-Indians. More than 3,000 volcanoes stood in Mexico, and earthquakes were frequent. Volcanoes, earthquakes, wars, and prolonged drought may have led prehistoric Mexicans to believe that evil forces lurked everywhere—in the skies, under the earth, and within the souls of men and women. They developed religious beliefs designed to protect them. The gods they worshiped loomed as heroes, soldiers, and father figures.

But the deities were strict patriarchs who demanded tokens of respect from their subjects. Sometime, deep in the past, the gods of Mexico began to require human life as a reward for working their miracles.

Earthquakes Still a Threat

September 15, 1985, dawned as a typical day in Mexico City. The sun rose and the usual traffic jams developed. Suddenly, high-rise buildings swayed. Great shards of glass fell from the buildings and rained down on the sidewalks. People shouted "*terremoto!*" ("earthquake!"). A powerful earthquake ripped through the Mexico City region, killing some 10,000 people and leaving thousands more homeless. The 1985 tremor was the deadliest earthquake recorded in Mexico in modern times.

Between 6000 BCE and 4000 BCE, the bands of hunters found a grass they could domesticate and cultivate into maize. Evidence suggests that the first maize was grown for human use near the city of Puebla, about 130 miles southeast of present-day Mexico City. There the people learned to plant seeds with sticks and nurture the corn into its full bloom. In all likelihood, the first agricultural societies in the New World began in Mexico. The practice of farming quickly spread to other parts of the American continent.

The Aztec History of Corn

The Aztecs, the last ancient Mexican people to thrive before the Spanish conquest, told their own story as to how men and women learned to grow corn. According to the tale, corn was once the exclusive property of the ants. Jealously, the ants kept the secrets of corn growing from humans. Then a god who loved humans disguised himself as an ant, entered an anthill, and carried out a kernel of corn, which he presented to humans as a seed. Thus, humankind discovered maize.

Corn became the staple food of the Mexican people. Staple foods are life-giving, as they can be stored and eaten in times of drought or during the winter. For Asians, the staple food was rice. European staples were wheat and barley. With corn, Mexicans lived longer and fewer babies died. Corn was eaten alone as a gruel or it was mixed with meat to form stews. Later, Mexicans developed ways to grind corn kernels and create tamales, and tortillas. The familiar pat-pat-pat sound of Mexican women hand-making tortillas from corn dough was first heard thousands of years ago. The distinctive sound can still be heard today in traditional households.

Metate and Mano

To grind corn and make dough for tortillas, the corn kernels were put on a stone slab (a metate) and crushed with a smooth stone (a mano). The two devices remain in use in Mexico, and they look and function as they did in ancient times. Today most corn is ground by machine, but Mexicans complain that the tortillas from machine-processed corn lack "the taste of the stone." Therefore, many people prefer tortillas made the old-fashioned way with corn ground by hand with a metate and a mano.

Puebloan women grinding maize between stones, as depicted in a hand-colored woodcut of a nineteenth-century illustration

The early farmers used the "slash and burn" method for cultivating their corn. They cut and burned the small trees and other scrub weeds growing from a patch of ground and planted seeds in the ashes. Because corn exhausts soil in just a couple of years, the ancient farmers cleared and burned new land, leaving the old patches fallow until the soil refurbished itself. Agriculture developed and new crops flourished. In addition to corn, the people developed ways to grow beans, avocados, squash, and the hot chili pepper.

Farming was a safer activity than hunting. Also, the ceaseless pursuit of food experienced by hunting societies moderated. People felt more certain that they would be properly fed in the weeks and months to come, so they spent more time on toolmaking and crafts. Devotion to agriculture allowed them to stay in one place and build village settlements. They erected pit houses with the floor dug below the ground. Archaeologists find the outlines of such homes in rocky areas today. Walls were made from pole frames interwoven with grasses and covered with clay. In the warm Mexican climate, such houses served the people well.

Some of the best farmland was found on the Central Plateau in a fertile valley that is about sixty miles long and forty miles wide. Present-day Mexico City lies on the valley's southern tip. Called the Valley of Mexico, the region today holds millions of people. The Valley of Mexico was a focal point in the nation's history during the earliest days and served as a cradle for many ancient societies.

Farming made it unnecessary for every person in a tribal community to contribute directly to food-producing activities. Some individuals became traders, others priests, others musicians and storytellers, and still others artists. By about 2000 BCE, the art of sculpture developed in Mexico. Skilled hands fashioned figures of turtles, ducks, deer, and fish. A popular piece was a clay statue four to six inches long of a woman. She is usually nude except for a headdress. Perhaps such female figures represented reproduction. Women may have prayed to them in hopes that the gods would grant them healthy babies. The small statues have been found by the hundreds in all parts of Mexico, and they now stand in museums.

Obtaining water to irrigate crops was an ongoing problem in all of Central Mexico because of the area's fickle rainfall. Near the present-day city of Puebla, the ancient Mexicans engaged in their most ambitious collective building project. Around 750 BCE, the people began building what is called the Purron Dam. Purron is the name archaeologists give to a period in Mexico's prehistory. It marked the first large-scale water management system in the New World. The dam created a lake in the Tehuacán River and allowed farmers to irrigate their lands in the dry months. With the benefits of irrigation, the people enjoyed two or even three crops a year. The dam was improved and enlarged, and it remained in use for more than six hundred years.

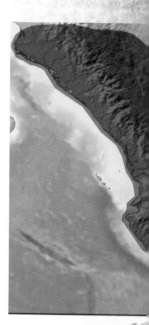

Farming villages rose in all parts of Mexico. We do not know the names of the villages, but certainly they had names. Trade was conducted from village to village and region to region. However, there was little mass movement of peoples. Mexico's ubiquitous mountains discouraged wide-scale travel on foot, and the country had no broad, smooth-flowing rivers that would accommodate rafts. Still, the people exchanged ideas and goods. Warfare declined, at least between farming communities. However, villages were subject to raids by bands of nomads who rejected farming and roamed the mountains and seacoasts.

Certain practices were common in most parts of Mesoamerica. The term *Mesoamerica* is used to describe a broad region stretching from Central Mexico south to Nicaragua. Mesoamerica, also called Middle America, was home to many advanced civilizations.

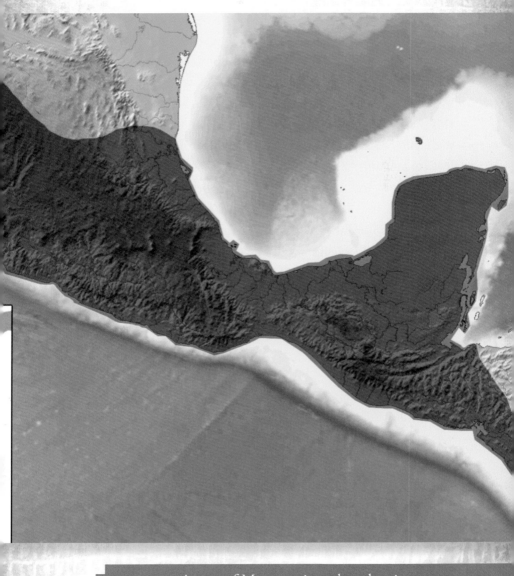

A map of Mesoamerica, a broad region
stretching from Central Mexico to Nicaragua

The people of Mesoamerica hunted and fished, but their diet was mostly vegetarian. They had no large animals, such as pigs or cattle, that they could slaughter for meat. They did keep turkeys and a breed of chubby dogs, and they ate the meat of these animals on festive occasions. Dogs, turkeys, and the honeybee were their only domesticated animals.

The Mesoamericans had no draft animals, such as horses or oxen, that could pull carts. Forms of horses and camels once lived in Mexico, but they died out with the mastodons. Therefore, all goods taken from village to village had to be carried on human backs. Without draft animals, the people had little use for the wheel. They used wheels only in jewelry creations and in children's toys.

Archeological evidence suggests that religion ruled the lives of ancient Mexicans. All tribes seem to have had a host of gods that granted rain, good health, success in marriage, victory in battle, and other favors. People in far-flung villages worshiped similar gods, indicating there was a lively exchange of religious ideas.

A ceramic urn portraying Cocijo, a pre-Columbian Zapotec god of rain, thunder, and lightning. Urns like this one were used by the ancient Zapotec people to honor deceased loved ones. Found at Monte Albán, the urn is on display in the National Museum of Anthropology in Mexico City.

Blood symbolized life in old Mexico. Bloodletting, the ritualistic drawing of blood in a temple, was a common practice. This was done with a knife made of razor-sharp obsidian or with the needle-like spine of a stingray fish. While a priest chanted prayers, a person giving sacrificial blood pierced a body part, bled freely, drained the blood into a bowl, and offered the blood to a statue of a god. Pictures on temple walls show men and women sticking pins into their tongues, earlobes, and genital areas. In one ritual, a man penetrates his tongue with a pin and then runs a string with thorns attached through the hole.

Human sacrifice, the ritualistic killing of human beings, was the ultimate form of worship. All ancient societies practiced some form of human sacrifice. The biblical story of Abraham, who came within a moment of sacrificing his son Isaac, is well known. Sometime in the past, priests in Mexico came to believe that the gods required human life to continue their work of protecting humankind.

A common form of human sacrifice, one practiced most often by the Aztecs, was to hold a person face-up over a sacrificial stone and cut his chest open with a knife. A priest then dug into the body with both hands, pulled out the still-beating heart, and presented it to a statue of one of the gods. In Aztec times priests told the victim that his gory death on the altar would propel his soul instantly to heaven in the afterlife.

An artist's impression of a jaguar, the symbol of the Olmecs, in the Tabasco region of Mexico

CHAPTER 2

The Olmecs

Archaeologists once believed that the Maya of southern Mesoamerica were the most advanced people in the New World. Historians have dated the start of Mayan culture at about 100 BCE to 200 BCE. However, Aztec scholars were aware of a people who once lived along the Gulf of Mexico in a place called *Tamoanchan*, or Land of Rain or Mist. There they studied the stars, built pyramids, and created huge statues. Aztec historians believed that the people fashioned a grand culture in ancient and legendary times. As an Aztec poet wrote:

> in a certain era
> which no one can reckon
> which no one can remember, where
> there was a government for a long time.

Today, we know that the people the Aztecs sang about were the Olmecs, a truly ancient and advanced civilization that lasted from 1200 BCE to 400 BCE. The word *Olmec* is Aztec for "rubber people." Those long-ago people produced rubber products, including a solid rubber ball for a ball game similar to soccer that was played throughout Mesoamerica. The name was later applied to the society that thrived along the Gulf of Mexico long before the rise of the Aztecs. We do not know what the Olmecs called themselves thousands of years ago.

The Olmecs built pyramids and carved marvelous statues long before the ancient Greeks constructed their great monuments on the other side of the Atlantic. Among their many accomplishments, the Olmecs developed the first system of writing in the New World. Olmec art and their philosophical and religious ideas influenced many later generations of Mesoamerica cultures, though to what extent is fiercely debated in Mesoamerican archaeology.

Olmec civilization rose principally along the Caribbean Sea in the present-day states of Veracruz and Tabasco. The region was a steaming swamp covered by jungles and host to swarms of mosquitoes. Mexico can be looked upon as a vertical rather than a horizontal country. The moderate and dry regions lie in the mountains and on the Central Plateau. A hot, humid, and rainy climate prevails at sea level on the two coasts. Even today, the states of Veracruz and Tabasco, home of the historic Olmecs, are among the rainiest places in Mexico.

The remarkable Olmec society was unknown to scholars until relatively recent times. The first hint of Olmec life came in the 1860s, when a sugarcane farmer in the state of Veracruz claimed he found a huge inverted stone pot or kettle buried in the ground near the Caribbean Sea. Several years later, a Mexican scholar named José Maria Melgar trekked into the swamps of Veracruz and discovered that the object in the mud was not a kettle at all. Instead it was the incredible statue of a stone head that weighed some ten tons. Melgar noted that the statue's face appeared to him to be "Ethiopic." In fact, Melgar proposed the idea that Africans had once visited the Gulf Coast of Mexico.

Gradually, other curious items not typical of Mayan culture were found in the Gulf region. In 1883, a decorative jade ax with a jaguar mask on its blade was uncovered. In 1909, an American mining engineer found the jade figure of a jaguar while he was leveling a mound of earth. The jaguar figure was so delicately carved that some observers speculated that it had been made in China. In 1929, Marshall H. Saville, director of the Museum of the American Indian in New York, published a paper in which he boldly stated that a culture distinct from the Maya once lived near the Gulf of Mexico. Saville called these people the Olmecs, and the name endured.

In 1938, American scientists from the National Geographic Society excavated the area where Melgar found the stone head decades earlier. They discovered a complex of pyramids that stretched some two miles. Because the pyramids were made of mud, they had deteriorated, but what remained indicated that a sizable city had once stood on those grounds. Amid the pyramid ruins, the researchers found an astonishing stone tablet that came to be called Stela C. This Stela, to everyone's surprise, had a date on its face. Using a bar-and-dot system of numbers (where a bar represented five years and a dot one), the researchers determined that Stela C predated the Maya by more than three hundred years. Here stood further proof that the Olmecs, not the Maya, had the first advanced culture in Mexico and Mesoamerica.

The Cascajal Block

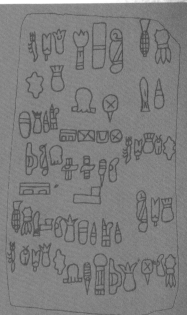

Evidence of the early Olmecs is still being uncovered in the Gulf of Mexico area. In 1999, a crew of road builders working near the city of Veracruz dug up a stone that appeared to be a slate with figures carved upon its face. There were sixty-two such figures representing animals and insects. In 2006, the highly respected *Science Magazine* announced that the Cascajal Block (named for a nearby archaeological site) was an example of Olmec writing, and that it was the oldest writing of any kind ever found in the Americas. Judging by pottery shards uncovered nearby, scientists dated the Cascajal Block at about 900 BCE.

An artist's sketch
of the Cascajal Block

Further investigation revealed that the ancient Olmecs were con- centrated around three major sites: Tres Zapotes, where the original stone head was found; La Venta, a religious center thirty miles to the south; and San Lorenzo, which was discovered years later and lies about midway between the first two sites. The three centers represented the ancient Olmec heartland. From this heartland, the culture spread in all directions.

The most spectacular works of Olmec art remain the great stone statues of heads. They are now called, appropriately, the Olmec Cal- losal Heads, and they still evoke wonders. How were they made? The Olmecs had no iron tools. Yet somehow their artists carved the distinct and fine facial features using stone implements. Fifteen Olmec Colos- sal Heads have been discovered; more may lie buried under ruins that have yet to be excavated. Most of the Colossal Heads are as tall as an average man, and they range in weight between ten and twenty tons.

Four such heads have been found at the La Venta site, which is a muddy island in the middle of a river. Basalt stone for the heads came from a volcano that rises about one hundred miles away. In an incred- ible effort, the ancient people dragged the enormous stone blocks over the soft soil of a rain forest and erected them on La Venta. Probably, they built rafts and floated the heads partway down rivers. However they accomplished this feat, it represents a remarkable moving job.

The facial features on all the heads are similar, so some researchers have concluded that they represent a certain class of people. Perhaps they were kings, perhaps gods. Many scholars believe that the faces are African, Chinese, or even Mediterranean. Skeletons do not survive when buried in this swampy land, so it is impossible to study the bones of the long dead Olmecs and determine their racial type. The statues all wear curious headdresses, which are also a mystery. One carving has been nicknamed "Uncle Sam," because it shows a man with a pointed beard.

The graceful jaguar fascinated Olmec artists. The Olmecs may have had a folktale that said at the beginning of time a jaguar mated with

One of the colossal Olmec heads in La Venta Park in Villahermosa, Mexico. The heads are thought to portray the mighty rulers of the Olmecs.

a woman and produced a baby that was half jaguar and half human: a were-jaguar. Large and small statues of were-jaguars have been found in Olmec lands. They have human bodies and feline faces. The faces show them snarling and even smiling. Often statues of the were-jaguars were carved with flat heads and an unusual v-shaped slit through the top of the head. In Olmec lore, jaguars must have mated with other animals too, and the result of this union can be seen in artistic masks fashioned by long-ago craftsmen. Some jaguar masks feature the feathers of a bird, while others have the tongue of a snake.

The Jaguar's Hiccups

Jaguars, which are now rare animals, once roamed the rain forest of Mesoamerica in great numbers. After lions and tigers, they are the largest members of the cat family. Nocturnal and shy, they rarely make contact with humans. Still, tales of their prowess were told and retold by Olmec storytellers, and those stories endured. In the 1500s, a native of the Gulf Coast told a Spaniard that, according to an ancient tale, the jaguar had a way of hypnotizing people by hiccuping. According to the native, hearing a jaguar's hiccups put a man into a frozen hypnotic state, thus enabling the animal to attack and kill him with ease.

The rare mineral jade was a favorite medium for Olmec jewelers and statue-makers. Deposits of jade, a stone with a rich green hue, are found in present-day Guatemala to the south of the Olmec heartland. Mexican scholar Ignacio Bernal stated, "The Olmecs were not only the first and finest sculptors of Mexico; they were the first to work jade and indubitably were the greatest in this medium. No other pre-Hispanic people were capable of producing the infinity of jade objects with the mastery of the Olmecs."

One particular statue, discovered by an early Spanish priest, was made from such a rare form of jade that it glowed in an almost mystical manner. The priest, Fray Benito, said, "The stone was so transparent it shone from within with the brightness of a flame. . . . [E]ngraved [on the stone] with the greatest skill [were] a small bird and a little serpent ready to strike." The bedazzling beauty of the carving and the richness of the stone proved too overwhelming for the priest. He suspected it was all the devil's work. Fray Benito pounded the statue to dust and then stamped on the dust in front of the natives "[in order] to destroy the heathen abomination and to show the impotence of the idol in the sight of all."

La Venta, the principal Olmec religious center, lies about ten miles from the Gulf of Mexico shore. Pyramid-building began there around 1100 BCE. This date means the Olmecs constructed pyramids even before King Solomon built his magnificent temple, which was exalted in the pages of the Bible. The primary pyramid, shaped like a volcano, rose to the height of a modern ten-story building. It faced a plaza at which worshipers once gathered.

There are no written records describing the religious meetings at La Venta, so we have to speculate as to the ceremonies that took place there centuries ago. The pyramids were flat on the top. Probably the priests stood on these truncated peaks to be closer to the heavens and to the gods. Perhaps drums pounded and flutes played while the priests chanted prayers to the gatherings below.

It seems that a certain amount of magic was mixed with Olmec religious services. Concave mirrors made of serpentine, a rock that reflects light when polished, have been found in Olmec temples. Sunlight directed from these mirrors can start fires at a distance or even project pictures. Yale University professor Michael Coe pointed out that "one can imagine the hocus-pocus which some mighty Olmec priest was able to perform with one of these."

Olmec statues, which were made of stone, have endured, but the pyramids of La Venta were of mud and soil and all have eroded. So, the site of La Venta is not impressive to the visitor today. Ages ago, the main pyramid in this complex was the largest human-made structure in all the Americas. One researcher estimated it took 800,000 man hours for a crew to construct La Venta's largest pyramid.

San Lorenzo is the earliest of the Olmec cities. Olmec-style buildings rose at San Lorenzo at a time when Rome and Athens were little more than farming villages. The buildings disappeared long ago, but impressive works in stone have been found in the ancient settlement. Huge stone altars, some weighing many tons, were once used in religious services at San Lorenzo. One altar features the figure of a man, probably a priest or a ruler, lovingly holding a were-jaguar baby.

San Lorenzo engineers eased the problems of their swampy environment by building an elaborate sewer system. Hundreds of U-shaped stones were carved out and placed alongside each other in drainage ditches to provide for water run-off. The sewage system functioned perfectly for centuries.

After 1200 BCE, life ended suddenly at San Lorenzo. Coe believes the city "was destroyed either by invasion, or revolution, or a combination of these." The great stone statues were smashed (sometimes decapitated) and then buried in long graves. Was this destruction ordered by a powerful priest, or did an outside army lay waste to the city?

Stone statues of an Olmec man and a jaguar at the
El Azuzal archaeological site near San Lorenzo, Mexico

No one knows. "Civilizations went out with a bang," Coe said, "not a whimper in early Mesoamerica."

At its height, an estimated 350,000 people lived in the Olmec heartland. The people hunted, fished, and farmed. The most productive Olmec farms lay along riverbanks that flooded at least once a year. Annual floods covered the soil with a rich layer of silt, which aided the growing of crops. Such regular flooding was also the key to Egyptian agriculture, which depended on the predictable overflowing of the mighty Nile River.

Theirs was not a peaceful society. Monuments depict Olmec warriors marching with clubs. One sculpture shows men brandishing clubs above the head of a frightened-looking man who may have been a prisoner of war. Some human bones that have been excavated show signs of butchering, indicating that the Olmecs occasionally practiced cannibalism. Bloodletting was an integral part of their rituals, as piercing devices such as shark fins have been discovered in Olmec temples.

The Olmecs were energetic traders. They sought jade, serpentine, and obsidian (a glass-like mineral used to make knives and spear points). None of these minerals were native to the Olmec heartland, so their trading parties traveled endless miles to obtain the desired goods. Olmec merchants exchanged their well-crafted artwork for the minerals they needed. Olmec-style art objects have been discovered as far west as present-day Mexico City and as far south as Costa Rica in Central America.

In addition to goods, the Olmecs spread religious and cultural ideas to other peoples. The Mesoamerican ball game, a sport similar to soccer, was first played by Olmec athletes who introduced the contest to their neighbors. Ball courts where the game was played are in many Mesoamerican ruins. Olmec architecture, especially the pyramid as a religious cathedral, became the standard in all of ancient Mexico.

Certainly the Olmecs told others of their gods. One god in particular, the Feathered Serpent, originated with the Olmecs and then took a long odyssey through the ages of Mesoamerican history. In later societies, the Feathered Serpent was a gentle god, but in the

Olmec version he is fierce. One Olmec statue shows the Feathered Serpent devouring a man.

Around 400 BCE, the Olmec civilization began to decline. It has been suggested that climate change, perhaps prompted by a particularly violent volcanic eruption, ruined their environment and made their soil impossible to farm for long periods.

Though their culture weakened, Olmec influence never died in ancient Mexico and Mesoamerica. Olmec art, philosophy, building, and engineering laid the foundation for subsequent societies, and their cultural footprints enabled future nations to thrive.

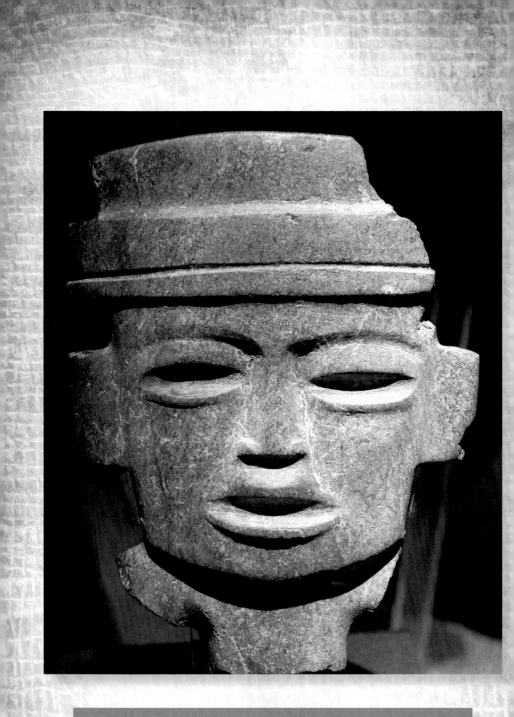

A stone sculpture of a chieftain's head excavated at Teotihuacán, the pre-Columbian archeological site near Mexico City

CHAPTER 3

The Mystery People and Their Mystery City

About seven hundred years ago, the Aztecs were a wandering tribe. While searching for a permanent homesite, they trekked into the Valley of Mexico. There they discovered the remains of a wondrous city. The nearly empty city, about thirty miles northeast of present-day Mexico City, had been abandoned hundreds of years earlier. The homeless Aztecs were awestruck pondering what a magnificent place it must have been! It had two great pyramids, a broad avenue running down its center, and dozens of lesser pyramids and apartment complexes. Walls on the outside of the buildings were bedecked with sculptures, and inside walls were alive with paintings. The Aztecs concluded that this fantastic city could not have been built by humans. Surely its creation was the work of gods. The Aztecs named the place *Teotihuacán*, or Adobe of the Gods.

Work of Giants

Near the ruins of Teotihuacán, the Aztecs discovered several half-buried mammoth skeletons that they believed to be the bones of huge human beings. This confirmed their belief in the supernatural origins of the city: The great metropolis was designed by gods and built by giants.

We now know that Teotihuacán rose early in the Classic Period of Mesoamerican history. The Classic Period (from 150 CE to 900 CE) was a golden age in old Mexico. It was a time when arts and science flourished and ancient societies such as the Maya, the Toltecs, and the Zapotecs built magnificent structures and soaring pyramids. But even by the high standards of the Classic Period, Teotihuacán was unique. It seemed that the people of the region got together and said, "Let's build a city." Teotihuacán was a planned city from the start, and it was the first large-scale planned city in all the Americas.

In olden times, before Teotihuacán was constructed, the Valley of Mexico held farming villages. The soil in the valley was fertile, but bountiful crops—then and now—were dependent on seasonal rain. Near where the city was to rise bubbled several springs, which were vitally important to the early inhabitants. Also significant was a natural cave that cut a path under what would become the city's tallest pyramid. Ancient Mexican traditions say that caves are the wombs of the earth, the places where all things are born.

Most of the valley's residents were farmers who also fished and trapped birds at nearby Lake Texcoco. The people worshiped at a pyramid called Cuicuilco, which had been built ages earlier. Then, in about 50 BCE, a volcano erupted, burying the sacred Cuicuilco Pyramid in lava and ash. A time of despair and darkness followed the eruption. Some stories said that the sun and moon had refused to appear and the stars had lost their glitter. The people believed that the gods had been angry and had ordered the end of the world.

The Cult of Cuicuilco

The pyramid complex of Cuicuilco has been excavated and can be visited today in a suburb of Mexico City near the National University of Mexico. The word *Cuicuilco* is often interpreted as "Place of Prayer." A cult has grown around the site, with some members believing that the major Cuicuilco pyramid is more than 7,000 years old. This would make Cuicuilco older even than the vaunted pyramids in Egypt. Most scholars dispute the 7,000-year-old-claim, but the pyramid is believed to be the oldest structure in the Valley of Mexico.

Adding fuel to the mystery is this story: During an excavation in the 1920s, a strange light appeared in the heavens one night directly over the Cuicuilco Pyramid, and it hung in the sky for several minutes before speeding off. Cultists later claimed that the light came from a UFO and that the incident proved that Cuicuilco had been built with the help of ancient astronauts.

The south side of the Cuicuilco pyramid located
in the Tlalpan borough of Mexico City

Centuries later, the Aztecs accepted the doomsday scenario associated with Cuicuilco, but they made up a story that had a happy ending. After a long spell of darkness and suffering following the volcanic eruption, the gods met at Teotihuacán to try to right the universe. An Aztec poem tells us:

Even though it was night,
even though it was not day,
even though there was no light
they gathered,
the gods convened
there in Teotihuacán.

One god, Nanahuatzin, the most humble of them all, decided to sacrifice himself in hopes that his death would restore life and happiness on earth. Nanahuatzin threw himself into a roaring fire and was consumed. He rose as the sun. Still, despite the rebirth of the sun, the other heavenly bodies did not return. So, one by one, the other gods sacrificed themselves until finally the universe began anew. Aztec lore always recalled that this miraculous return to life took place at Teotihuacán.

To celebrate the recreation of the universe, the people of the valley decided to build a city. In their dreams, it would rise to become the most glorious city in all the world. Its buildings would be constructed strong and huge in order to defy natural calamities such as earthquakes and volcanic eruptions. Thus, they began work on what the Aztecs hundreds of years later called the Abode of the Gods.

Engineers and work crews concentrated on the most ambitious project first: building the tall pyramid that today is known as the Pyramid of the Sun. That pyramid rose directly over the cave that was thought to be holy in ancient times. It was not until 1971 that modern researchers found the cave, and we still do not know about its true significance. The Aztecs believed that the sun, moon, and stars were reborn on this spot because of the will of the gods, and perhaps the

The Pyramid of the Sun at Teotihuacán, outside Mexico City. Built over a natural cave with four chambers, the pyramid is the third largest in the world, standing behind the Great Pyramid of Cholula, also in Mexico, and that of Giza, in Egypt.

cave acted as a heavenly womb. The Pyramid of the Sun was designed to evoke awe, and it does so to this day. Its base is as large as the Great Pyramid of Giza in Egypt, but the structure itself is about half as tall. The Pyramid of the Sun had a flat top, which held a temple. The building and its temple served as a grandiose center for religious worship.

Site Names

Outstanding features of Teotihuacán include the Pyramid of the Sun, the Pyramid of the Moon, the Avenue of the Dead, and the Temple of the Feathered Serpent. All these names were given to the sites by the Aztecs and retold to the Spaniards. We do not know what the original builders and residents of the city called their structures and their streets.

To the north rises the Pyramid of the Moon. It is not as tall as the Pyramid of the Sun, but because it rests on sloping ground, the Moon building's peak is about the same height as that of the Sun. The Pyramid of the Moon is a delicate, pleasing structure best viewed from the special Moon Plaza at its base. The broad Avenue of the Dead begins at the Pyramid of the Moon. It runs past the Pyramid of the Sun and to the Citadel (a name given to a plaza area by the Spaniards because they thought a fort once stood there) and the Feathered Serpent Temple.

Teotihuacán: Still a Wonder

Today, the ancient city of Teotihuacán thrills visitors as it did the Aztecs hundreds of years ago. Lying about a forty-five minute bus ride from downtown Mexico City, it is the most visited archeological site in all of Mexico. Tourists climb to the top of the Pyramid of the Sun and behold a magnificent view of the city from its peak. The top of the Pyramid of the Sun is flat, and a temple that was probably made of wood once stood there. No trace of that temple remains. The Pyramid of the Moon is not as high, but the steps are taller and their slant steeper; climbers are advised to take their time. The peak of the moon pyramid allows one to look the length of the Avenue of the Dead—a stunning sight. As tourists make their way up the pyramids, they muse about the mysteries here: How was this massive city built? Why? And why was it so suddenly abandoned?

Nothing was laid out by chance in Teotihuacán. The Pyramid of the Moon rises in line with a mountain behind it (today called Cerro Gordo, the Fat Mountain). The residents of Teotihuacán apparently believed that Cerro Gordo was the source of their spring water. The Avenue of the Dead runs straight for about a mile until its course adjusts slightly to align with the constellation Pleiades, a cluster of seven stars also known as the Seven Sisters. The Pleiades constellation is important to the Mesoamerican calendar.

Construction began on the first stage, the Pyramid of the Sun, at the start of the Common Era. For the next several centuries, work on the city never ceased. We do not know how many construction workers labored on the building projects, but the crews undoubtedly made up a small army. No draft animals or wheeled carts were available to move material. Everything was carried on workers' backs in a scene that must have resembled human ants building a giant hill. Construction continued in several stages until the city's completion in about 650 CE. Thus, most of the building took place in the Classic Period, when Mesoamerican civilization flourished.

Upon completion, the city spread over eight square miles and held as many as 200,000 residents. Professor Coe estimated that it was the sixth-largest city in the world in 600 CE. Most of its residents worked as farmers, but evidence suggests they lived within the city rather than residing near their fields. This meant that farm workers had to make long walks to and from their farms each morning and evening. It is not known whether farmers were required by authorities to live in city dwellings. Perhaps the excitement of city life lured the farmer folk inward and they gladly endured the walks.

Aside from its farm population, Teotihuacán was devoted to industry. It could be said it was the first "factory town" in the Americas. The Avenue of the Dead is misnamed because in its heyday it had to be the liveliest street in the city. On each side stood workshops and family dwellings. Potters in the shops made their goods with a material called "thin orange." Fashioned from a special orange clay, cups, plates, and pitchers made in this style were as thin as eggshells. Yet thin, orange pottery items were strong, and most were gaily decorated. The potters of Teotihuacán put their imagination into their products. Some cups were made to resemble human feet, and jaguar or dog figures appeared on bowls.

Excavations have revealed that about 2,000 workshops of various kinds operated at Teotihuacán. Some shops were devoted to weaving cotton clothes, while others made leather products from animal skins.

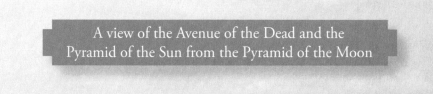
A view of the Avenue of the Dead and the
Pyramid of the Sun from the Pyramid of the Moon

At least 350 of the shops produced obsidian tools. With no iron available, the natural glass obsidian was valued throughout Mesoamerica. Obsidian came from a nearby mountain that was later called Cerro de las Navajas, or Knife Mountain. The obsidian from Knife Mountain was black in color, like most obsidian, but it had a hint of green. Knives made from this material, worked by the skilled hands of Teotihuacán's toolmakers, were traded to far-flung communities. Ceramic figurines made by Teotihuacán artisans have been found. These treasured items were buried with kings in many places in Mexico and even as far south as Honduras in Central America.

Teotihuacán's favorite trading partner was the city of Cholula, which lay about eighty miles to the east. The people of Cholula were ethnically similar to the people of Teotihuacán. Cholula was founded in about 400 BCE, and it is speculated that at various times the same king or kings ruled over both Cholula as well as Teotihuacán. In the center of Cholula rises a great pyramid that is larger than anything in Teotihuacán. When the Spaniards arrived in the 1500s, this pyramid was long abandoned and so overgrown with earth and vegetation that it looked like a tall hill. The pyramid still looks more like a hill than a human-made structure, and today many buildings including several churches stand upon it.

Excavations have shown that Cholula's giant pyramid was built over another ancient, pyramid-like structure. On the inside wall of the earlier pyramid is a famous mural called *The Drunkards*. The painting shows men toasting each other with beakers believed to contain pulque, the cactus beer of Mexico. Tradition says that pulque-drinking was permitted only on festival days, and it seems that the men portrayed in the mural are enjoying their festivities.

Teotihuacán's workers lived with their families in apartments, which were neatly separated by streets and alleys to form neighborhoods. The city-dwellers lived the first true urban lifestyle in the Americas. Olmec cities predated Teotihuacán, but they were more places of worship than they were places to live. Housing units in Teotihuacán were comfortable and surprisingly egalitarian for the times. Ruling-class men and women of Teotihuacán did not live vastly richer lives than did the average worker. In fact, little is mentioned about kings or high priests lording over Teotihuacán. However, it is known that the lords and the priests enjoyed a far more varied diet than did the commoners. Meat was a dish eaten almost exclusively by the rich. The rest of the people had to be satisfied with a vegetarian diet augmented perhaps by a taste of dog or turkey meat on festive occasions.

Curiously, nowhere in the vastness of Teotihuacán have archaeologists found an understandable written word that dated back to antiquity. Certainly they were a literate people. No city as grandiose as Teotihuacán could be built if engineers were unable to convey their ideas to workers without written orders. Tiny pictures of birds' beaks being held by human hands and jaguars in human dress have been found, and it is reasoned that these are actually writing glyphs. However, no modern scholar has been able to read the Teotihuacán ancient language, if such a language indeed existed.

The sculptors of Teotihuacán did not carve magnificent statues like the Olmecs did. The city's most evident statues are those of angry-looking serpent heads that poke out from the outside walls of pyramids. But certainly not all of Teotihuacán's statues were designed to frighten people. Smaller figurines, often made with pottery material, show lightness and gaiety. Masks were a favorite subject for Teotihuacán artisans, although it is not certain how these masks were used. Did people simply hang them on the walls, or did they hold the masks in front of their faces while dancing at grand fiestas?

Teotihuacán's artistic brilliance burst forth in paintings. Murals (wall paintings) are seen everywhere on inside walls. It could be said that Teotihuacán was a painted city. Even the walls of the humblest working-class families were covered with murals. Often, the wall paintings depict the people at work or at play. A famous Teotihuacán mural, called *Tepantitla*, has been recreated and now is displayed at the National Museum in Mexico City. The Tepantitla painting shows men and women at a river, where they are bathing, fishing, and chasing butterflies that are as big as themselves. The people appear to be singing as

The Paradise of Tlaloc, one of a series of murals found in 1942 in the Tepantitla compound in Teotihuacán. The murals depict scenes of everyday life in ancient Teotihuacán, and in *The Paradise of Tlaloc* people are shown diving and swimming in a river with fish, eating, talking to each other, and picking flowers. The strange looking curved shapes in front of the people are speech bubbles, which signify that they are talking or chanting.

they play, and—almost like a modern comic strip—word balloons appear to emerge from their mouths.

Plentiful water, and the happiness that an abundant water supply brings, is a common theme in the city's murals. This comes as no surprise considering the semi-desert climate of the Central Plateau. Drought in the plateau region is a constant threat to life and prosperity. The Teotihuacán rain god, whom the Aztecs called Tlaloc, is a prominent figure in many of the wall paintings.

With no understandable written language to study, we must turn to the pictures on walls to try to understand how the city-dwellers lived. Unlike most Mesoamerican cities, no ball court exists in Teotihuacán, but we know they played the traditional ball game because a mural shows the athletes in action. In the ballgame mural, the athletes propel the ball along with sticks, similar to modern field hockey. None of the paintings are signed or show any identity with the artist. It is as if the murals belong to all the people viewing them and the painter is just the bearer of gifts.

A detail from *The Paradise of Tlaloc* shows a man playing with a ball.

Religion was central to the lives of Teotihuacán residents. Featured among the city's gods is the Spider Woman (her mouth looks like that of a spider complete with fangs), who represents the creation of humans. Always, the Rain God is present in Teotihuacán's religious art, along with the Water Goddess and the Fire God. Much religious art is devoted to the Fire God, who had the important job of carrying the sun across the sky during the course of the day. The Feathered Serpent continues his march through ancient Mexican history in the Teoti-huacán pantheon; the city's third-tallest pyramid is dedicated to this powerful deity.

Teotihuacán's religious rituals included human sacrifice. In a mass grave under the Pyramid of the Feathered Serpent lie some two hundred sacrificial victims. They did not die willingly. Their hands were tied behind their backs and their feet tied together. Some were strangled while others, it appears, were buried alive. Often, sacrificial victims in Mesoamerican culture went to their deaths in relative peace, believing they would soon be propelled into the heavens and become companions to the gods. The victims buried under the Pyramid of the Feathered Serpent had to be forced into accepting their grim fate. Many conclude that the bound men were prisoners of war who invaded the city in ancient times.

Belief in life after death was universal in the city. The afterlife world was thought of as a pleasant place where no one experienced thirst or hunger. Few graves have been found in Teotihuacán because the people favored the cremation of the dead. Still, the Aztecs believed the city was both a tomb and a paradise, as can be seen in this Aztec poem:

> And they called it Teotihuacán
> because it was the place
> where the lords were buried.
> Thus they said:
> "When we die,
> truly we die not,
> because we will live, we will rise,
> we will continue living, we will awaken.
> This will make us happy."

The mystery city thrived for more than seven centuries. Then it died a mysterious death. Reminiscent of the Olmec fate, Teotihuacán was deliberately destroyed. In about 700 CE, many of the city's statues were smashed and its wooden temples burned. The destruction was most evident in the heart of the city, near the Pyramid of the Sun and the Pyramid of the Moon. Was the city sacked and burned by an outside army, or was the devastation caused by an internal upheaval? This is a riddle that perhaps will never be solved.

We do know that the city's influence over its neighbors waned during its last stages, before its final death. Starting in 600 CE, fewer Teotihuacán-made goods appear among its favorite trading partners. Various theories are advanced to explain the city's sudden weakness. One theory lay in the cement used to construct the massive buildings. That cement (mortar) was produced by burning limestone blocks. This process required huge fires, and workers had to cut down thousands of trees in order to produce fires that generated the mortar. Without tree roots to hold the soil in place, erosion laid waste to land surrounding Teotihuacán and made farming far more difficult. Another theory holds that the city attracted more people than the rain-starved land could feed. The population tripled between 100 BCE and 650 CE, and it is quite possible that famine set in. Teotihuacán was, therefore, a victim of its own success.

The city was never completely abandoned. Warrior bands from the north moved in, haunting the ruins like ghosts. But pyramid-building stopped, and the magnificent products that once flowed out of its shops ceased to be made.

The legacy of Teotihuacán shaped Mexico in its Classic Period, the nation's ancient Golden Age. Art, architecture, philosophy, and religion born in Teotihuacán reached out and touched the genius of later societies, challenging future generations to achieve their own greatness.

Mayan calendar

CHAPTER 4

Time
and the
Maya

In the beginning, according to a Mayan creation myth, there was only the sea and the sky. No soil, not even a rock, existed anywhere. One god lorded over the sky and another deity ruled the sea. The two got together and simply whispered the word earth, and soil as well as mountains appeared. Next, the two gods created all the animals. They hoped the animals would have the gifts of speech and understanding so they would obey orders and make proper sacrifices. But, to the gods' dismay, the animals could not speak nor could they understand words. So the two gods created people. After several failed attempts—one unsatisfactory version of humans was made from mud and another from wood—the supreme beings finally created the human race as it exists today.

Mayan liturgy contains many such myths and legends, and we can understand them today thanks to the Maya's gift for writing. No society in all of ancient America had as complete a writing system as the Maya did. Their writing was a complex mix of both glyphs and symbolic pictures. Only in the last twenty or thirty years have scholars learned how to properly decipher the Mayan written language. Professor Michael Coe stated that "as much as 85 percent of the total body of classic Mayan inscriptions can now be read. . . . This means that the ancient Maya are now the only truly historical civilization in the New World, with records going back to the third century after Christ."

Burning Books

The Maya wrote inscriptions on temple walls and on stone stelae. They also wrote in books made from tree bark or deer skin. The pages of their books were lavishly illustrated with different colored inks, often showing pictures of gods interacting with people. Only four of those ancient Mayan books (codices) have survived. Spanish priests went to the Mayan lands in the 1500s and burned every book they saw because they believed the codices held the work of the devil. A particularly zealous book-burning priest was Diego de Landa, who wrote to his superiors in Spain, "We found a great number of books in these letters of theirs, and because they contained nothing but superstition and the devil's falsehoods, we burned them all."

Mayan culture developed in the Central American countries of Belize, Guatemala, El Salvador, and Honduras and spread to Mexico. Within present-day Mexico, the Maya rose in the southern states of Campeche, Yucatan, Qintana Roo, Tabasco, and Chiapas. At the height of their civilization, the Maya occupied more than 120,000 square miles of Mesoamerican territory, and Mayan kings ruled over more than 22 million people.

Their history began around 1000 BCE, in what scholars call the Preclassic Period. At that time, the Olmecs to the west were building their remarkable society. There is no doubt that the powerful Olmecs influenced the Maya. The hot, humid jungle climate of Guatemala was similar to that of the Olmec homeland. The Guatemalan rain forest, complete with swarms of mosquitoes, was not a pleasant place to build an advanced culture. Not only was the land a swamp, it was sometimes plagued by periodical droughts. Vanderbilt University scholar Arthur Demarest said of the Mayan region, "A high civilization had no business being there." But the Maya, sometimes called the Lords of the Jungle, thrived in this rather uninviting land. Given time, Mayan civilization reached even greater heights than did the Olmec culture.

Mayan art, architecture, and sculpture still fascinate us today. In the sciences, the ancient people reached fabulous heights. Their scholars were mathematical geniuses who created the most accurate calendar in use anywhere in ancient times. Mayan mathematicians were the first in the world to use the concept of zero. In Mayan picture writing, a zero is shown with a picture (a glyph) of a seashell. Interestingly, in addition to zero, the Maya also had a single glyph or mathematical unit that represented the number 64 million.

The Mayan people reached their greatest height during the Classic Period (roughly 150 CE to 900 CE) of Mexican history. During that era they built stunning cities, including Tikal in Guatemala and Palenque in Mexico.

Tikal thrills visitors even now, more than 1,000 years after the city reached its zenith. Tourists today ride a bus down a jungle road and then approach on foot two pyramids soaring above the treetops. The pyramids face each other, separated by a plaza that runs about the length of a football field. These two structures, popping out of dense jungle growth, serve to confirm the Mayan status as masters of the rain forest. Only the central part of this great city has been restored. Beyond the two pyramids are housing and religious sites still covered by jungle growth. Excavation is a continual process at Tikal, and it is likely that even more surprises will someday emerge from this marvelous Mayan site.

The Tikal National Park

The ruins of Tikal stand in the Tikal National Park in northern Guatemala. The park spreads over 222 square miles of rain forest, which contains many other remains of Mayan civilization. Tikal National Park is managed by the University of San Carlos in Guatemala. The university's scientists are carefully excavating Mayan sites while they preserve the beauty and the ecology of this rich jungle. The parklands are home to spider monkeys, howler monkeys, and the rare jaguar.

The pyramids of Tikal follow a Mayan pattern that is evident in most of their ancient cities: Many of the structures were built over even older buildings. Mayan architects, it seems, were never satisfied with a finished product. They kept building and rebuilding so that newer pyramids covered older ones like layers of an onion.

At its zenith, more than 100,000 people lived in the Tikal region. The question looms: How did this land, which is essentially a swamp, feed such a large population? Mayan engineers solved this problem by creating raised fields. Workers covered swampland with flat stones and then piled freshly dug soil upon the bed of stones. Canals were dug out along the sides of the raised fields to allow excess rainwater to run off. Corn, squash, and beans grew abundantly on the raised fields. Tikal farmers not only fed the local population, but they produced enough excess crops to trade with neighbors for other goods.

The Maya of southern Mexico did not live in a swamp. Water was scarce in the Mexican areas, especially in the present-day state of Yucatan. Ancient people in the Yucatan grew what food they could and

The main plaza at the ruins
of Tikal in Guatemala

concentrated on trade as their main economic activity. Yucatan farmers raised honeybees and mined salt to use as trade items. The Yucatan region was the greatest producer of salt in all of Mesoamerica. A lively trade took place between Yucatan merchants and the farmers of Tikal. Trade goods were transported by fleets of canoes, which skirted the Caribbean coast. Instead of money as we know it, the Maya exchanged cacao beans, copper bells, and pieces of jade or silver. Colorful bird feathers were also objects of value.

The Dinosaur Killer

In truly ancient times, an earth-changing event took place near the Yucatan Peninsula in southern Mexico. For more than 160 million years, dinosaurs were the most dominant creatures on the planet. Then, about 65 million years ago, the great beasts went extinct in a relatively short period of time. Why? Today, scientists believe a huge asteroid the size of Mount Everest slammed into our planet near what is now Mexico's Yucatan Peninsula. The impact caused an explosion as powerful as 100 million hydrogen bombs. This immense blast threw clouds of dust and soot into the sky, blocking out sunlight, killing vegetation, and causing the death of 75 percent of all of earth's animals—including the dinosaurs. Scientists accepted this dinosaur-killing collision theory in recent years

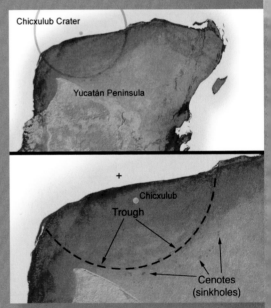

Radar topography reveals the 112 mile diameter ring of the Chicxulub crater. Clustered around the crater's trough are numerous sinkholes, suggesting a prehistoric oceanic basin in the depression left by the impact.

when an enormous impact crater, called Chicxulub, was discovered by satellite photos in the Caribbean Sea off the Yucatan coast.

Chíchen Itzá was a major Mayan city in the present-day Mexican state of Yucatan. The city was built around a great well, which was actually a sinkhole formed when the roof of an underground cave collapsed, exposing a submerged river. Many such sinkholes are found in Yucatan. The holes were called *dzonots* by the Maya and later *cenotes* by the Spaniards. They were vital sources of water for the Yucatan Maya, and at times they became places of sacrifice. Valued items and even human beings were thrown into the *cenotes* in order to please the gods so they would continue to allow life-giving water to gush through the underground rivers. In the Mayan tongue, Chíchen Itzá means "at the mouth of the well of Itza."

Sacrifice at the Well

Spanish priests visited the well at Chíchen Itzá long after the Maya stopped sacrificing human beings there. The priests reported that in the old days young girls, chosen for their beauty and grace, were the preferred sacrificial victims. The girls were thrown into the well at sunrise. Most drowned. But if the girls survived by splashing about the waters until midday, they were taken out and questioned by priests. The priests wished to know if, during their struggles, the gods gave them any special messages.

Trade enriched the people of Chíchen Itzá, and the city rose to become one of the most powerful centers in the Mayan world. Today Chíchen Itzá, with its soaring pyramids and finely carved stelae, is the second most visited archaeological site in Mexico—second only to Teotihuacán.

The Maya have been called the Greeks of the New World, and in some ways the comparison is valid. Like the ancient Greeks, the Maya lived in city-states that acted independently. Sometimes the Maya city-states waged war on each other, as was true with the city-states in Greece of the bygone era. Also similar to the Greeks of old, the Maya were devoted to arts and sciences.

El Castillo (the castle) is the common name given to the Mesoamerican step-pyramid that dominates the center of the Chichén Itzá archaeological site in the Mexican state of Yucatán.

The passage of time fascinated Mayan thinkers and priests. Their obsession with time has, in turn, fascinated researchers who study their ancient works. Writing in 1950, British scholar Sir Eric Thompson noted, "I conceive the endless progress of time as the supreme mystery of the Maya religion, a subject which pervaded Maya thought to an extent without parallel in the history of mankind."

To satisfy their hunger to understand the workings of time, the Maya looked to the sky. Their scholars plotted the course of the moon and the planet Venus in order to fashion the special Mayan calendar, a precise system of measuring and recording time. The calendar they created was the most accurate in the world. Its development required a gift for astronomy and mathematics.

The Mayan calendar incorporated a system in three parts. Part one was a religious calendar called the *Tzolkin*, which highlighted special days set aside to honor certain gods and goddesses. A second calendar, known as the *Haab*, had 365 days and was used by farmers to determine the best time of the year to plant or harvest crops. The Haab was based on the orbit of Earth around the sun, and it made adjustments for leap year. The third calendar, today called the Long Count Calendar, measured eras of almost unimaginable length. Each Long Count era was 5,126 years.

Transposing the Maya Long Count system with the Gregorian Calendar that we now use, we can make an interesting—and perhaps scary—conclusion. According to Long Count calculations, our present era began August 11, 3114 BCE; it is scheduled to conclude on December 21, 2012.

Does the Maya Long Count Calendar mean the world will come to an end in 2012? Many present-day researchers on the Maya say the 2012 date simply marks the beginning of a new epoch, the turning over of another Long Count. But students of astronomy point out that in December of 2012, the sun will line up precisely with the center of our Milky Way Galaxy. This is a rare alignment that happens only once every 26,000 years. The Maya were among the greatest astronomers in history, and it is possible they found something worrisome about the year 2012.

One of the Maya Codices ends on an ominous note. The last page of the *Dresden Codex* (so called because it surfaced many years ago in Germany) shows a dragon with water gushing from its mouth and a goddess emptying water from a pitcher. Some observers believe this means the world will be destroyed by a great flood occurring on December 21, 2012.

The Maya played the Mesoamerican ball game with great zeal. Ball courts stood in the center of most of their major cities. It is still not known exactly how the ball was propelled the length of the field. Players were not allowed to kick the ball or grab it with their hands. Points were scored when a player put the ball through a hoop that was attached to a wall, as one would do while playing modern basketball. Scoring had to be low. The inner hoop on surviving ball courts is not much

Page 49 of 74 of the *Dresden Codex*, the most complete of the remaining codices. The codex contains astronomical tables, agricultural almanacs, and predictions for the future based on the alignment of the planets and the stars.

larger than the outer diameter of the ball. The Maya, always given to astronomy, compared the movement of the ball with the course of stars as they made their way through the night sky. The game also had religious overtones. Sometimes the captain of the losing ball team was sacrificed to the gods.

Mayan society was changed by a visit from a mysterious stranger. Inscriptions call the visitor Fire-Is-Born and claim he arrived in the Maya lands in January 378 CE. Soon his name would appear on monuments in practically every Mayan city. We now believe Fire-Is-Born came from Teotihuacán, some one thousand miles to the north over the twisting roads. Either he brought an army with him or he recruited an army, for he quickly conquered the powerful city of Tikal and became its king. For the next three hundred years, the culture of Teotihuacán influenced the Maya. Art and architecture took on Teotihuacán qualities. Teotihuacán gods appeared in the Maya pantheon. For reasons we fail to understand, the Maya became a more violent people after their close association with Teotihuacán. Warfare between the city-states intensified, and the practice of human sacrifice became more frequent.

Religious art shows that earlier in Mayan history their gods were satisfied with animals as sacrificial objects. Bloodletting was part of their rituals, but it was primarily kings and other royal family members who punctured a body part with thorns and offered their blood to the gods. Then came Fire-Is-Born and the sway of Teotihuacán. Suddenly, the Mayan gods demanded the lives of human beings. War prisoners, slaves, and even children were offered up to the altars. It was primarily unwanted children who were slaughtered to please the deities.

The Maya, as was true with all Mesoamerican people, believed in a life after death. They carefully buried their dead, wrapping corpses in straw mats and painting them red. Funeral services for Mayan leaders were grand affairs, which sometimes called for human sacrifice. Slaves and servants were sacrificed and buried with their king in order to serve him in the afterlife.

The world of the dead was not a pleasant place. The Maya underworld, which a person entered at death, was called *Xibalba*, or Place of Fright. The underworld was made up of several layers or floors upon which different forms of torture were practiced. Heroes of the underworld were twin brothers who, while on earth, played the Mesoamerican ball game and were so noisy with their giggling and shouting that they disturbed powerful gods. The gods sentenced the twins to death. But the twins were clever and managed to find a comfortable niche, even in hell. By worshiping the twins during one's life, a person could escape some of the torments of the Maya underworld.

The Day of the Dead

Pondering the afterlife is a passion in modern Mexico, at least on one day each year. Every November 2 is celebrated as the *Dia de la Muerte*, or Day of the Dead. On this special day, family groups gather at the grave of a loved one. They clean the grave, plant flowers, and perhaps sing the dead person's favorite song. The Day of the Dead is not at all a somber time. Instead, it is a holiday during which people remember loved ones and reflect upon death as a natural event—one that will eventually happen to everyone.

In about 700 CE, the Mayan civilization declined rapidly. Drought and overpopulation likely contributed to the sudden collapse. City-states in the lowlands of Guatemala were the first to be abandoned. The highland Maya, those who lived in Mexico's Yucatan region, remained strong for centuries after the lowland people deteriorated.

By the time the Spaniards came in the 1500s, Mayan society was a shadow of its ancient glory. Yet the people were never truly conquered. Despite the presence of Spanish overlords, the Maya continued their old ways and practiced many aspects of their old religion. The Maya live today in southern Mexico and northern Central America on virtually the same territory they occupied centuries ago. Often they identify themselves as Maya first and Mexicans or Guatemalans second.

A statue found at Monte Albán in Oaxaca during
excavations of the large pre-Columbian archaeological site

CHAPTER 5

The People
of
Monte Albán

Most pyramids in Mexico were built with a flat top. Such truncated peaks represented an effort on the part of the people and the priests to reach to the heavens—the gods. Temples stood on the level pyramid peaks. Astronomers studied the stars, priests prayed there, and human beings were sometimes sacrificed on the lofty heights. This pattern makes Monte Albán in southern Mexico unique. Monte Albán is not a pyramid. It is instead a mountain fashioned to look like a pyramid.

In ancient times, armies of workers flattened the peak of Monte Albán to create a vast ceremonial platform. How they did this staggers the imagination, as the mountain is as high as a modern ten-story building and has steep sides. The construction project was undertaken with stone tools and without the aid of draft animals, machines, or wheeled carts. Even drinking water had to be carried up the sides, as there is no source of water anywhere on Monte Albán. Yet the ancient construction crews succeeded in turning a mountain into a pyramid.

Touring Monte Albán

The archeological site of Monte Albán lies about a fifteen-minute bus ride from the city of Oaxaca. Every day, hundreds of people arrive to tour the ruins. The flattened area of the mountain covers almost one square mile. It contains pyramids, temples, decorated tombs, a ball court, and a broad plaza. The top of Monte Albán also offers a sweeping view of the Oaxaca countryside.

Monte Albán rises in the Y-shaped Valley of Oaxaca (pronounced *wah-HAH-cah*), which lies about four hundred miles south of Mexico City. The Valley of Oaxaca is a fertile region in the middle of rugged mountain chains. Today, Oaxaca is one of Mexico's thirty-one states; its capital is the charming city of the same name.

The valley attracted people in early times. An Oaxaca village, today called Teotitlan del Valle, is one of the oldest human settlements in all of Mexico. It is not known why the ancient people chose Monte Albán to be their focal point, nor is it known what they called the mountain. Monte Albán is a Spanish name and comes from a wealthy Spaniard who once owned the property.

A panoramic view of Monte Albán, which was built
around 500 BCE and flourished until 750 CE

Some archaeologists have suggested that Paleo-Indians used Monte Albán as a military fortress because its peak gave observers a commanding view of an approaching enemy. A military function is hinted at in one of the monuments on the top. A series of stone reliefs called the *Danzantes* (Dancers) shows naked men who, many scholars believe, are being forced to dance in order to humiliate them before putting them on the altars to be sacrificed. The dancing men appear to have Olmec features, and they were carved late in the Olmec era. Historians and scholars conclude that a battle between the Olmecs and the local tribes took place at Monte Albán. The Olmecs lost the battle, and their captured soldiers suffered a horrible fate. In the artists' carvings, all the nude dancing men are mutilated in some way, many by being slashed in the groin area. Blood flows freely from their wounds. The carvings on stone slabs stood as a grisly warning to potential enemies: do not invade us!

Monte Albán was the home of the Zapotec and later the Mixtec peoples. Both groups still live in the region, and many speak their native languages in addition to Spanish. The Zapotec culture is one of the oldest in Mexico.

Even today, when a Zapotec is asked how long his or her family has lived in the Oaxaca region, he or she might smile and say *siempre* (forever). Farmers speaking the Zapotec language began cultivating fields there as early as 1500 BCE. Zapotec farming villages stretched out for hundreds of miles in Oaxaca, but Monte Albán was the people's governmental and religious center.

Archaeologists have determined that ancient workers began leveling the top of Monte Albán as early as 500 BCE. Temples and the other religious buildings were constructed in stages on the flattened peak over the centuries that followed. The religious nature of the site cannot be overlooked. One of its possible ancient names translates as "Hill of the Sacred Stones." The abundance of tombs on the mountaintop suggests that it was a holy spot. The tombs, which most likely held the remains of powerful leaders, are elaborately decorated and consist of rooms connected to other rooms. Murals cover the walls on most of the tombs. Fine examples of pottery have been found there, placed near the deceased. Sometimes dogs were buried with the Zapotec dead because a Mesoamerican belief holds that a dog can lead a person to a more pleasant part of the underworld.

The Whistling Jar

One interesting Zapotec pottery piece found near Monte Albán is called the whistling jar. This was a jar with two chambers connected at the bottom. When water was poured into one chamber, air was forced out the other. That flowing air made a whistling sound as it passed through a special valve on the top.

Only high priests actually resided on the sacred mountaintop. The lack of water alone discouraged a large population on the peak. Most of the people lived on the level valley floor, where they tended to farms. Monuments on the mountain peak were stuccoed and brightly painted.

The Zapotecs were farmers, architects, builders, artists, and craftspeople. At the height of their civilization, around 700 CE, their nation embraced some 250,000 people and spread out over eight hundred square miles. Monte Albán remained their capital, but it was not their only city. One major settlement was at Mitla, located about twenty-four miles from today's city of Oaxaca. Mitla was known in ancient times for manufacturing brightly colored tile. Another important town, today called El Palmillo, held a castle that consisted of twenty rooms.

Master Weavers

The Zapotecs were the greatest weavers in Mesoamerica. In ancient times, they fashioned colorful cotton clothing that was valued by their neighbors and served as trade items. The Spaniards introduced wool to the people in the 1500s, and they soon mastered this material too. Fine weaving is still an outstanding Zapotec industry. Zapotec weavers today are famous for creating superb rugs and wall hangings.

The Zapotecs believed in a supreme being who created the universe, but they never made an image or statue of this almighty god. They did create hundreds of statues, carvings, and pottery pieces of the more earthly gods. Cocijo (a Zapotec word for "lightning") served as their rain god. Pecala was their god of love and the giver of pleasant dreams. They worshiped their deceased ancestors, especially those of royal blood. Above all, they worshiped nature and believed that anything that moved—even the winds and the clouds—had life and spirit.

Around 750 CE, power declined in the Oaxaca region. The people quit building monuments, and slowly the religious center at Monte Albán lost its lordly population. The Zapotec nation had thrived for almost 1,200 years. Why its strength waned is a mystery, like so many other aspects of ancient Mesoamerica. However, as was true with the Maya before them, the Zapotecs preserved their ways of life and spoke their old language even after the Spaniards conquered Mexico.

Monte Albán, a UNESCO World Heritage site,
commands sweeping views of the Valley of Oaxaca.

As the Zapotecs weakened, a new people—the Mixtecs—rose to prominence in the Monte Albán region. The Mixtecs lived in the jagged mountains of western and northern Oaxaca. They were sometimes called the Cloud People because of their highland homes. They formed valley settlements where they were ruled by kingly families. The Mixtec language had many variants, and it was difficult for the people of the various villages to speak to each other. Apparently, the Mixtecs enjoyed more or less friendly relations with their Zapotec neighbors. While it is true that the Mixtecs eventually took over Zapotec lands, they accomplished this feat because their royal family members married their Zapotec counterparts. Such noble marriages limited fighting between the two cultures.

Miraculously, four Mixtec books, or codices, survived the Spanish conquest and exist today to be studied by scholars. The codices were written on deerskin, and to read them one must unfold the pages like road maps. Mostly, the deerskin books documented the lives and deaths of leaders and recorded important marriages. However, one codex tells of the culture's origin. According to the codex, the Mixtecs sprang forth, as if they were fruit, from the branches of a tree at a place called Apoala. The book gives no hint as to the location of this magical birthplace.

Mixtec pottery and sculpture works rival that of the Zapotecs. Mixtec artisans were among the first in Mesoamerica to use metals in their jewelry creations. Employing gold, silver, and turquoise,

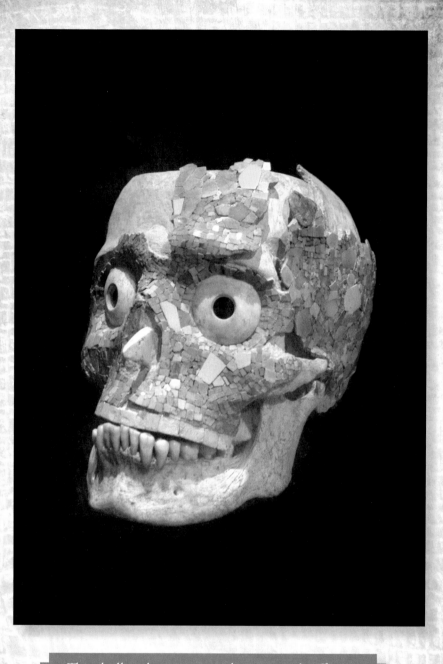

This skull with turquoise inlay is a tomb offering, uncovered from one of the tombs at Monte Albán.

Mixtec jewelers created fine pieces that they often buried in the tombs of their leaders. As the centuries passed, the Mixtecs built their own royal tombs on Monte Albán. One particularly handsome Mixtec tomb was excavated and found to contain exquisitely carved gold pendants as well as necklaces comprised of hundreds of pearls.

The most famous Mixtec leader was called Eight Deer Jaguar Claw, who reigned after the fall of the Toltecs. This great king expanded Mixtec territory through marriage and through conquest. A codex said he married at least five times. Each marriage resulted in the takeover of new lands, villages, and subjects. He was not a pleasant in-law in his new family circle. Often he had his wives' parents sacrificed. Ultimately, Eight Deer Jaguar Claw met a violent end himself when he was killed by a family member of one of his many wives.

Today, the Mixtecs and the Zapotecs still live side by side in Oaxaca. Each July, the state holds a grand fiesta, the *Guelaguetza*, featuring parades with bands and marchers wearing bright costumes. As is true with so many Oaxaca events, the fiesta is a blend of Catholicism and the ancient religions. Oaxaca has more indigenous-speaking people than any other state in the Mexican Republic.

An artist's impression of Tenochtitlán, capital of the Aztec empire

CHAPTER 6

Mexico in the Classic Period

The Classic Period of ancient Mexican history lasted from 150 BCE to 900 CE. It was a time when cultures flourished and then mysteriously disappeared, and new cultures with fresh ideas rose to their zeniths. The great societies of the Classic Period—the Maya, the people of Teotihuacán, the Zapotecs, and others—are relatively well known to students. Smaller, lesser-known groups also reached lofty standards of achievement in Classic times. The Classic Period was one of intellectual and creative energy. Late in the Classic Period, however, angry gods appeared in Mexican pantheons and nations grew more militaristic.

Pre-Columbian Mexico

The 1492 voyage of Christopher Columbus marked a major turning point in the history of Mexico, effectively ending the country's ancient period. Columbus himself never set foot on Mexican soil, but his expedition to the New World set the stage for other Europeans, especially the Spaniards, to arrive. The Spaniards brought a new religion, a new language, and hundreds of different institutions to the New World. Therefore, Mexican history is divided into Pre-Columbian (ancient) and Post-Colombian (modern) times. Historians, including Dr. Michael Coe, further divide the Pre-Columbian era into subperiods, as shown below:

Archaic

Archaic Period (before 1800 BCE): The spread of agriculture occurs.

Preclassic

Early Preclassic (1800 to 1200 BCE): The Olmec civilization develops.

Middle Preclassic (1200 BCE to 400 BCE): The Olmecs rise to prominence in the Gulf of Mexico region.

Late Preclassic (400 BCE to 150 CE): The Pyramid of the Sun is built in Teotihuacán and the Maya invent the Long Count calendar.

Classic

Early Classic (150 CE to 600 CE): Work begins on Monte Albán.

Late Classic (600 CE to 900 CE): The city of Teotihuacán and several other important civilizations decline.

Postclassic

Early Postclassic (900 CE to 1200 CE): The Toltec state is formed.

Late Postclassic (1200 CE to 1521 CE): The Aztecs rise and dominate central Mexico until the Spanish conquest.

Cholula, the city in central Mexico associated closely with Teotihuacán, achieved its greatness in the Classic Period. The Great Pyramid at Cholula rose as high as a fifteen-story building, making it perhaps the tallest structure anywhere in the New World during the Pre-Columbian era. Over the years, several cultures occupied Cholula, and the city outlived nearby Teotihuacán. Trade was a primary activity for the Cholulans. Objects made in the Mayan lands and in shops at Monte Albán have been found in the city. In the Late Classic Period, Cholula somehow lost its vigor. Building stopped in outlying districts, and dirt and brush covered the Great Pyramid. Foreign invasion is likely a reason for its downward slope.

During the Classic Period, trade remained active in most of Mexico. Without horses, the trading parties traveled on foot, carrying goods on their backs. The trading parties of old Mexico were large and employed men trained from boyhood to be bearers of cargo. In the isolated villages, where the people rarely saw strangers much less unusual goods, the arrival of a trading band was an exciting event. Even those who had no goods to trade came to examine the strange and often exotic merchandise. The Aztecs claimed that traders who traveled from afar were highly respected people, and laws stated that to rob or cheat them was an especially serious crime.

Goods made in the Monte Albán region continued to be valued in other parts of Mesoamerica. Beyond the year 700, the Mixtecs held sway at Monte Albán, and their craftsmen were pioneers in working with metals. The Mixtecs won the reputation as the finest goldsmiths in ancient Mexico. Gold was valued not so much because it was a rare metal, but because in skilled hands it made statues and jewelry of dazzling beauty. The Mixtecs also crafted copper items such as axeheads and delicately carved small bells.

The rather sudden appearance of copper and gold is another testament to the advanced trade practiced in ancient Mexico. Often these metals came from far to the south, in present-day Peru and Ecuador. They were transported to Mexico on boats and overland by trade caravans.

Chichén Itzá, one of the longest lasting of the Mayan cities, survived into the Late Classic Period. Mayan civilization eroded first in the Guatemalan jungles to the south. Many Mayan citizens then moved north to Mexico's Yucatan region, where Chichén Itzá is located. The city thrived as the newcomers poured in. Merchants in Chichén Itzá traded in obsidian and gold. By 700, Chichén Itzá was a lively regional capital.

The city of El Tajín, in the Veracruz region, began in the Early Preclassic Period and reached its zenith in Classic times. From 600 CE to 900 CE, El Tajín was one of Mexico's leading cities. A legend says that twelve old men once lived on the site and controlled the thunderstorms that so often lashed Mexico's Gulf Coast. During the Classic Period, the city center was striking, dominated by a sixty-foot stepped pyramid. All the structures in the heart of the city were stuccoed and painted a bright red. Apparently, these city dwellers loved to be entertained. As many as nine ball courts have been uncovered at El Tajín. In addition to the ball game, evidence suggests that human sacrifice was a frequent public event within the city. Dr. Michael Coe wrote, "Above all, the inhabitants of El Tajín were obsessed with the ball game, human sacrifice, and death."

Field of Walls

The ball courts in ancient Mexico are often shaped like a capital *I*, with two sloping walls running along each side in the middle of the letter. In pictures, these walls look like bleacher sections where fans sit to watch the game. Actually, they were not seating areas at all. They were instead part of the playing field. Competing teams were required to move the ball, somehow, along the slopping walls in order to score a goal.

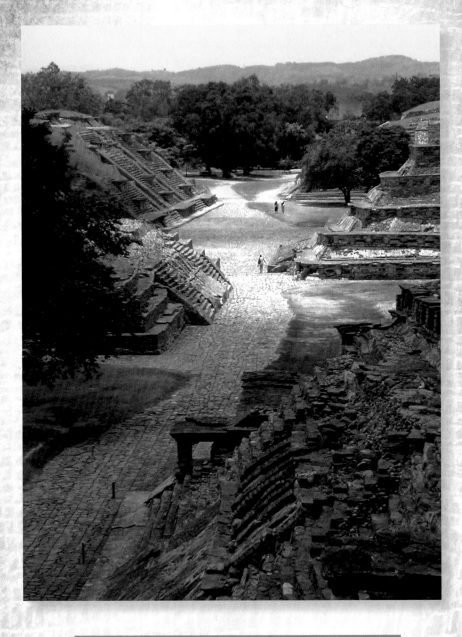

The ruins at El Tajín in Veracruz, Mexico

In sharp contrast to the boisterous people of El Tajín were the Totonacs, who also lived in the Veracruz region. Ancient writers praised the Totonacs for their friendliness and their gracious manners. They were traders who took boats up and down the Gulf Coast to exchange goods with others. Perhaps, as salesmen, they had to cultivate proper manners. Politeness served them well, because the culture lasted for hundreds of years. In 1520, the Spaniards landed in what is now Veracruz, and the Totonacs were one of the first Mexican groups they encountered. The Totonac chief promptly made friends with the European invaders.

Despite many advances, the Late Classic Period (from the years 600 to 900) was a time of unrest and warfare. Nomadic groups from the north began raiding the great cities. The nomads were called the Chichimeca, which can be translated as "barbarians." They had no written language and no advanced arts or crafts. For generations, the Chichimeca camped on the borders of cities such as Teotihuacán and Cholula and remained there as outsiders who wanted in so that they too could enjoy the comforts of urban life. The settled people always viewed them with fear and disdain. Armies kept the Chichimeca at bay, but when the cities' social structure collapsed their fighting forces lost power. As a result, the Chichimeca flooded into the cities. They often lived in the ruins of what were once stunning pyramids and palaces.

Historians have argued why this general decline took place all over Mexico, starting in about 700 CE. Drought, soil exhaustion, warfare with the Chichimeca, or possibly the outbreak of epidemic diseases are theories put forth for the downturn. Internal rebellion is another possibility, as farmers grew weary of working in the fields as well as constructing palaces for kings and pyramids for gods.

Drought combined with diminished irrigation certainly must have caused suffering and hunger in central Mexico. The mountainous regions of the country always required irrigation to keep the crops growing. Mexican engineers were skilled in designing water-holding dams, but irrigation systems could not be built without large crews of laborers. When the political power of cities such as Teotihuacán diminished, leaders could no longer organize small armies of farmers and direct them to build dams.

Central Mexico suffered a sharp loss of population despite the arrival of hoards of Chichimeca coming from the north. In the Valley of Mexico, the population dropped to about 150,000, or a little more than half the number of people living there in Teotihuacán's heyday. People fled hunger and died due to disease brought about by a woefully inadequate diet.

All over Mexico, the huge societies of the past divided into petty kingdoms with jealous, warlike leaders. The Chichimeca joined these kingdoms with sometimes good and sometimes disastrous results.

After 700, as food production lessened and the "barbarians" invaded cities, the deities more and more showed their furious faces. For the first time, the skull rack—the dreaded *tzompantli*—made its appearance in Mexico. *Tzompantli* were sets of shelves specially designed to hold the severed heads of sacrificial victims. Rows of gruesome-looking heads, with their empty eye sockets staring into eternity, served to remind the gods that the people were generous in their offerings. A Spaniard saw one of the chilling racks in the Aztec capital and wrote that it was "full of skulls and large bones arranged in perfect order, which one could look at but not count, for there were too many of them."

A section of the Wall of Skulls (Tzompantli), in Chichén Itzá. This sacrificial platform is where the Mayan displayed the heads of their dead enemies.

A chacmool statue holding an offering for the gods at the Great Temple of Mexico City

CHAPTER 7

The Toltecs: Warrior/Poets

Strongest of the Chichimeca groups were the Tolteca-Chichimeca, who originated in the north. They evolved into the Toltecs, who dominated much of Mexico from the years 900 to 1200. The Toltecs spoke Nahuatl, a language that was common in central Mexico and was also spoken by the Aztecs. Perhaps the Toltecs were the original Nahuatl speakers. Their writers composed poems and songs praising their gods. The written Nahuatl language does not convey emotions well, but we know many Toltec legends through oral traditions. Toltec storytellers told their tales to the Aztecs, who in turn told them to the Spaniards.

The Aztecs believed that the Toltecs of old were a race of supermen, heroes in every way. Toltec epic poems telling of the deeds of gods and warriors were ingrained in Aztec literature, and the poems were taught in their schools. The older culture was idolized by the Aztecs in much the same way as Europeans esteemed the Greeks and their Golden Age. Aztec lore even said that Toltec farmers grew miraculous crops, such as ears of corn so heavy that only a strong man could lift them, and they harvested cotton that sprouted in bright colors—any color the grower desired.

Toltec was a Nahuatl word meaning "builders," and architecture was their greatest strength. The Toltecs constructed their capital, Tula, in the Valley of Mexico about fifty miles north of present-day Mexico City. At its height, the city covered five square miles and held more than 30,000 people. In the ninth and tenth centuries, after the collapse of Teotihuacán, Tula was the largest city in Mesoamerica.

At the center of the Toltec capital stands a pyramid complex surrounded by plazas, ball courts, and palaces. On the flat top of the largest pyramid rise columns that at one time held the wooden-beamed roof of a temple. The columns, each about fifteen feet tall, are carved in stone relief to represent soldiers. They stand stiffly as if in ranks, and today they are called the Stone Warriors. Grim-faced men, armed with spears, they represent the martial spirit of the Toltec nation.

Tula Today

The ruins of Tula lie about a one-hour bus ride from Mexico City near the modern village of Tula de Allende in the state of Hidalgo. The long-ago Toltecs called their capital Tollan, meaning "where people are thicker than reeds." Tula was a widely known ancient city, but major excavations were not started there until the 1930s. Excavations were complicated by the fact that the Aztecs got there first. The Aztecs so idolized the Toltecs that in the 1400s they looted many of Tula's statues and columns and moved them to their capital. Touring ancient Tula, one can stand face to face with stone warriors.

Tula's massive stone warriors, standing nearly fifteen
feet high, once supported a wooden temple roof.

Toltec society rose in Early Postclassic times, when the nations of
Mexico grew militaristic. Exactly why this wave of militarism swept
Mexico is unknown, but the Toltecs were torchbearers during these
harsh times. Led by their army, the Toltecs expanded their borders to
include all of the Valley of Mexico, and their influence spread south
down to the Mayan lands of Yucatan.

Chíchen Itzá and the Toltecs

The outstanding Mayan city of Chíchen Itzá in the Yucatan is likely one of the Toltec conquests. Scholars debate whether such a Toltec invasion ever occurred, because Chíchen Itzá lies almost a thousand miles from the Toltec capital. But clearly two forms of architecture stand out at Chíchen Itzá. One form is Mayan, built in the seventh century. The other form shows a Toltec influence and was constructed from the tenth century to the beginning of the thirteenth century. Prominent in the newer architecture are columns with carved reliefs of armed soldiers, similar to those in Tula. Other sculptures represent altars decorated with human skulls.

Human sacrifice was a dramatic as well as frequent event in Toltec society. Some of the most prominent statues found at Tula are the *chacmools*, half-reclining figures with their knees bent and their heads turned to one side. On the belly of a typical Toltec *chacmool* was a bowl designed to hold offerings for a god. On religious festival days, priests filled the bowls with human hearts.

Cannibalism was widespread among the Toltec society. Enemy soldiers captured in battle were most desired because it was believed that eating the flesh of a warrior transferred his courage to the person feasting upon him. The Toltecs reverently buried their own dead under the houses they once owned, but they threw the remains of those whom they cannibalized onto refuse heaps.

The Toltecs excelled in engineering. Crews built a series of dams along the Tula River to furnish water to farmers. The Spaniards found these dams still functioning even after five hundred years of use. The fact that leaders could assemble small armies of workers to construct irrigation systems suggests that a strong political organization existed in the Toltec nation. In Late Classic times, the power of many states had dwindled to the point where leaders no longer were able to assemble men and direct them to complete public works projects.

The Aztecs claimed that the Toltecs were the world's greatest crafts-men, but most scholars today conclude that their arts were inferior to what was produced in Monte Albán and in Teotihuacán. Toltec statues, though impressively large, appear joyless and even scary. Some of their sculptures depict eagles with human hearts in their beaks. On oth-ers, snakes are shown eating human beings whose skin has been flayed from their bodies. British-born archaeologist Brian Fagan asserted that the Toltecs were "a battle-scarred, militaristic civilization, one in which oppression was a way of life and human sacrifice second nature, a far cry from the golden age of Aztec legend."

The Toltec people worshiped at least one gentle god: the enigmatic and complex Feathered Serpent. The Feathered Serpent first appeared in Mexico in Olmec times, and centuries later a huge temple was built in his honor at Teotihuacán. In central Mexico, he is sometimes de-picted in sculpture as a rattlesnake with the wings of a bird. The Toltecs gave him a distinctive name: Quetzalcoatl. *Coatl* means "serpent" and *quetzalli* means "green feathers."

Is Quetzalcoatl a legend? Was he a lord? Was he a man and a ruler? Depending on the story one reads, he was all these things, and his mul-tiple roles render his legacy in Mexico confusing.

In one text, Quetzalcoatl was a man born to a tenth-century Toltec king. When he was an infant, his father was murdered by his brother, Quetzalcoatl's uncle, who then seized the Toltec throne. Immediately after the murder, Quetzalcoatl's mother fled Tula with her small son. In exile, the boy was sent to school in the city of Cholula, where he astounded his teachers with his brilliance. As a young man, he returned to Tula, fought his uncle, and finally threw him into a sacrificial fire. Thus, Quetzalcoatl avenged his father's murder and became king of the Toltecs.

Once on the throne, Quetzalcoatl loomed as both a ruler and a teacher. He taught his people metalworking and showed them new agricultural techniques. The office of a king also made him a judge, and in that capacity he was gentle with his subjects. Often he forgave crimes rather than meting out harsh punishments.

A stone carving of a feathered serpent head decorates the Temple of Quetzalcoatl in Teotihuacán, Mexico.

King Quetzalcoatl issued an important decree: under his rule, human sacrifice was banned in the Toltec nation. He said the gods were to be given flowers and butterflies as gifts rather than human hearts. His decree infuriated a rival god named Smoking Mirror, and it angered many priests who delighted in ripping open the chests of sacrificial victims. The priests, so the legend goes, tricked Quetzalcoatl by getting him drunk on cactus beer and inducing him to make love to a beautiful girl. When Quetzalcoatl woke up from his drunken stupor, he realized he had committed a grave sin. In remorse, he gave up the Toltec throne and escaped east to the Gulf of Mexico.

At this point, several tales merge and the grief-stricken Quetzalcoatl becomes a god. He was the god of wind and was represented by the planet Venus. According to the godly tales, Quetzalcoatl sailed into the Atlantic Ocean on a raft made of snakes woven together like straw. Before he left, Quetzalcoatl vowed that he would return and claim all of Mexico as his realm. He even gave a return date: the year One Reed on the Mexican calendar. On the European calendar, One Reed translated to 1519, a significant year in Mexican history.

The Toltec nation was short-lived by Mesoamerican standards, lasting only two hundred years. At its height, the Toltec Empire spread over central Mexico and extended to both coasts. This vast empire provided a degree of unity in early Postclassic times when Mexico had divided into dozens of small kingdoms, each jealous of the others. When Toltec society finally ended, in about 1200, its death throes were typical for Mesoamerica: the capital city, Tula, was sacked and burned by invaders. Most historians believe that the invaders were "barbarians" from the north.

Despite the Toltecs' passion for war, artistic splendor added glory to their civilization. Toltec architecture and poetry move us even today. It is no wonder that the Aztecs hailed the older Nahuatl-speaking culture as divine. A Nahuatl poet, surveying the ruins of the great city of Tula, wrote this farewell song:

> Everywhere there meets the eye,
> everywhere can be seen the remains of clay vessels.
> of their cups, their figures,
> of their bracelets,
> everywhere are their ruins,
> truly the Toltecs once lived there.

The Aztec god of rain and agriculture,
Tlaloc, from the *Codex Vaticanus*

CHAPTER 8

The Rise
of the
Aztecs

The collapse of the Toltecs once again left ancient Mexico leaderless. For years after the Toltecs declined, no society came forward to unite Mexico and to provide direction. Then, in the 1400s, the Aztecs rose in the Valley of Mexico. The Aztecs were the last great Pre-Columbian culture, and in many respects they were the most dynamic people ever in Mesoamerica. They were a society formed in the Postclassic Period, and—typical of the times—the Aztecs were devoted to military triumph and to their gods. They were also remarkable builders, organizers, and poets.

According to their own legends, the Aztecs once lived in a Mesoamerican Garden of Eden. It was a wonderful place to the north called Atzlán, or Land of the White Herons. In Atzlán, the weather was always perfect, the streams teemed with fish, and waterfowl glided gracefully above crystal clear lakes. An ancient text states, "There [the Aztecs] feasted on great numbers of ducks of all kinds, storks, sea crows, and water hens. . . . They gorged themselves on a variety of great and beautiful fish. They rested in the cool shade of trees that grew on the water's edge."

By all accounts Atzlán was a heavenly place, but the Aztecs' time there was short. Somehow the people insulted a mighty god, who expelled them from this paradise. The legend does not give details regarding their offense, but they were turned away from Atzlán as surely and as permanently as Adam and Eve were cast out of the biblical Garden of Eden. Beyond the gates of paradise, nature—once so beneficial—became the bane of the Aztecs. "[L]ater," says the text, "when they left this delectable land, everything turned against them. The underbrush bit at them, the stones scraped them, the fields were filled with burrs and spines . . . and were impassable, with no place to sit and rest."

Where Was Aztlán?

The word *Aztec* means "People from Aztlán." The Aztlán experience was vitally important to the ancient society. All Aztec children were taught the Aztlán legend in their schools. However, it was unknown if Atzlán really existed or, if it was an actual place, where it was located. Questions regarding Aztlán puzzled Aztec scholars even in Pre-Columbian times. Deep in the past, the Aztec government sent an expedition north to search for Aztlán, but the party returned after finding nothing resembling the American Eden. Modern theorists have placed ancient Aztlán a few hundred miles north of present-day Mexico City, and some claim it lay as far away as the American state of Wisconsin. Aztlán—myth or realty—remains an interesting riddle of the past.

For centuries after they were ousted from Aztlán, the Aztecs wandered the deserts of northern Mexico searching for a home. The tribe had scant water supplies, and for food they ate snakes, lizards, and even grasshoppers. During their quest, the people acquired a god named Huitzilopochtli, meaning "Hummingbird on the Left" in the Nahuatl language. They carried the Hummingbird's wooden statue in a cage-like device, and it was believed their priests could speak to the figure. The god told the priests to seek out a place where they would see an eagle perched on a cactus while eating a snake. On that spot, they should build a city. That city, the god promised, would grow to become the capital of a mighty nation. The god gave them a general direction: in their search, they should always keep the Gulf of Mexico toward their left hands. Hence, the god's name—Hummingbird on the Left.

After a trek that tribal historians claim lasted centuries, the wandering people entered the lush and fertile Valley of Mexico. The huge valley, which encompassed some 2,700 square miles, stunned the Aztecs. Never had the desert nomads seen a place such as this. Trees towered into the sky, and farmers' fields were green with corn. Compared to the deserts of northern Mexico, this indeed was the Promised Land. However, the Aztecs were uninvited guests. The settled people in the valley regarded the newcomers with deep suspicion. An ancient writer reported, "And when the [Aztecs] arrived here . . . they were the very last to come into the valley, and nobody knew of them or welcomed them, and everywhere people asked who are these people and where do they come from, and they were turned away from every village."

Aztec historians wrote that their people arrived at the Valley of Mexico about one hundred years after the fall of the Toltecs. Central Mexico at the time held six major city-states, which were constantly at war with one another. The region's chronic warfare played into the hands of the homeless Aztecs. Generations of wandering and defending themselves against other tribes had toughened the people, making them splendid warriors. So, they hired themselves to the various city-states as mercenaries, soldiers who fought for pay. One city-state after another employed the Aztecs to fight its battles. The Aztec army showed a talent for slaughter and quickly gained a reputation as a fearsome fighting machine. But none of the people who paid the mercenaries trusted them, because it was believed that the Aztecs were treacherous by nature.

One prince who hired the Aztecs was named Achitometl, the ruler of a state called Colhuacan. He allowed the band to camp at Tizapan, a rocky area no one wanted because it was infested with snakes. To the prince's surprise, the Aztecs appeared to be delighted by Tizapan.

The one-time desert dwellers moved onto the grounds and quickly killed and feasted on the snakes. Next, the Aztecs asked Achitometl if his daughter would serve as their queen and also participate in a religious service in which she would become the bride of their god Huitzilopochtli. The prince agreed, and the daughter was led away by Aztec priests. Later, the prince entered a hastily constructed Aztec temple and was horrified to see a priest dressed in the bloody skin of his daughter. She had been sacrificed to the Hummingbird, her skin was stripped off her body, and it was given to the Aztec priest to wear as a costume. The enraged prince drove the Aztecs out of his territory.

Once more the Aztecs were doomed to wander, but shortly after the bloody event at Tizapan they experienced a revelation. On a muddy island in the middle of Lake Texcoco, the people beheld a long-awaited vision: they saw an eagle sitting on a cactus while eating a snake. The promise of their god was fulfilled. According to Aztec historians, the miracle of the cactus occurred in the year 1325 on the western calendar. The Aztecs immediately began building a city that they named Tenochtitlán, Place of the Cactus.

Modern Mexico City

Ancient Tenochtitlán is now Mexico City, capital of the Republic of Mexico. The spot where the Aztecs claim they saw their divine vision is today the city's famous public square, the Zócalo. This plaza is flanked by the tall Municipal Cathedral and the elegant National Palace, the center of government. The government of Mexico officially lists 1325, the year of the vision, as the founding date for Mexico City. The symbol of an eagle sitting on a cactus while devouring a snake is at the center of every Mexican flag.

First, the Aztecs worked to expand their island settlement. Engineers directed construction crews to drive wooden pilings into the lake bed close to the shore and form a wall surrounding the island. Workers then piled mud from the lake bottom between the wall and the shore. After completing one such wall, they repeated the process, and the island grew outward in stages like the rings of a tree. Since they were a military society, this enormous construction project proceeded in a steady and disciplined manner. No one questioned an order from a superior. Laborers worked to the point of exhaustion and beyond without complaint.

The Aztecs were not innovators. They brought no original ideas in art, architecture, or religion to the Valley of Mexico. Instead they learned engineering and construction techniques from the settled people who they had so carefully observed during the years when they were outsiders. Once in command of their own destiny, the Aztecs showed a particular genius to create institutions that were uniquely their own. With tireless energy, the once rootless people built the mightiest empire in Mesoamerica.

As their island expanded, workers constructed a stunning city on its surface. It was a planned city based on what they had seen in the ruins of Tula and at Tenochtitlán. Towering pyramids and luxurious palaces for the royalty rose in the city center. Arrow-straight canals were dug to allow boats to bring in goods. Streets were laid out in a grid-like fashion. Four causeways, wide enough to allow ten people to walk abreast, were constructed connecting the island city with the distant shores of Lake Texcoco.

Instant Aristocracy

The Aztecs continued to believe that the Toltecs were the greatest society in Mexico's past. The Aztecs thought—wrongly—that it was the Toltecs who created the marvelous city of Tenochtitlán. At one point, early in their history, Aztec scholars discovered a man who they believed was a distant relative of a powerful Toltec priest. The Aztecs gave the man a house and twenty wives and told him to have many babies. The offspring of this arranged multimarriage became the future blue bloods of Aztec society. They served as an instant aristocracy for the young nation.

After more than a century of furious work, Tenochtitlán stood as a dream-like metropolis. The Aztec capital was an urban wonderland like nothing else that existed in the world. Drinking in the beauty of the capital city, an Aztec poet wrote:

> The city is spread out in circles of jade,
> radiating flashes of light like quetzal plumes.
> Beside it the lords are borne in boats,
> over them extends a flowery mist.

Providing food for the city-dwellers was a challenge for Aztec farmers and engineers. At its zenith, the city of Tenochtitlán held as many as 250,000 people, making it bigger than any city in Europe at the time. Lake Texcoco, home to the island-city, lay in a bowl-shaped depression. Therefore, it was impossible to dig canals and gravity-feed water to farmers' fields. So, the Aztecs did the reverse by bringing fields to water. Workers drove timbers in square-shaped formations into the lake bottom. They then scooped soil into the squares, creating farming plots. Trees were usually planted along the sides of the plots to give them greater strength. Sprouting trees and plants, the small fields looked like floating islands. The farms-in-the-lake were called chinampas, and in

A hand-colored nineteenth century woodcut reproduction of an early Spanish colonial map of Tenochtitlán, the capital of Aztec, Mexico

sunny Mexico they provided two or even three crops a year. The last such chinampa in the Valley of Mexico is Mexico City's Xochimilco, today a park and a tourist attraction.

The Aztec genius for engineering also provided drinking water for the people of the capital. Lake Texcoco had a salt content that made its waters suitable for irrigation but not for drinking. Aztec engineers designed an aqueduct composed of two huge pipes that ran three miles from a spring on Chapultepec Hill to the heart of the city. The pipes, each about six feet in diameter, were elevated on posts, allowing boats to pass easily beneath them. Tenochtitlán's aqueduct was the finest such system found anywhere in the New World.

With Tenochtitlán as its base, the Aztec Empire expanded in all directions. First the Aztecs subdued the smaller city-states in the Valley of Mexico. At one time, the Aztecs were an outcast tribe, shunned and feared by the settled societies in the huge valley. Now the people who once looked upon the Aztecs in disgust were forced to accept their rule. Beyond the Valley of Mexico, Aztec-controlled territory extended to both coasts and spread north to the barren deserts and south to present-day Guatemala. By the early 1500s, the Aztec Empire measured some 100,000 square miles, and the lords of Tenochtitlán ruled as many as 12 million people.

The Aztecs acquired this vast domain thanks to a ruthlessly efficient army, an institution that was a cornerstone of their society. Dr. Michael Coe said of the Aztec military, "The main goal of the Aztec state was war. Every able-bodied man was expected to bear arms, even the priests and the long-distance merchants. . . ." Aztec boys were born to be soldiers. When a midwife delivered a male baby, she was required to place a toy spear and shield in the infant's hand and chant an oath: "This place where you were born is not your true house, because you are a soldier. . . . You are promised to the field of battle."

In all, about 370 city-states in Mexico fell under Aztec sway. Some of the city-states were invaded and conquered by Aztec soldiers, but many simply gave up without a battle. The Aztec army was a splendid and terrifying sight. Officers wore feathered headdresses, which towered above the ranks. Soldiers marched to the beat of drums and the wail of trumpets. Before going into battle, the army units performed wild war dances. Many city-state leaders saw this fighting force at their gates and surrendered at once, rendering whatever price they had to pay in tributes in order to avoid invasion.

A detail from the Stone of Tizoc, a carved round stone in which scholars believe the hearts of sacrifices were placed. In the frieze are fifteen pairs of figures, each of an Aztec warrior holding his captive. The stone is located in the National Museum of Anthropology in Mexico City.

All Aztec males attended military schools before graduating into the army. Boys from the working classes were sent to institutions, where they were taught to march and to fight with clubs. Discipline within the schools was harsh, and punishments were expected to be self-imposed. A boy who broke the rules was obliged to stick himself with a thorn in the earlobe, tongue, or genitals. Boys from ruling-class families went to even stricter schools called the Calmecacs, or Houses of Pain. Students at the Calmecac were forced to bathe in icy waters and hike for many miles.

As teenagers, Aztec boys reported to the army to serve as novice soldiers. Their heads were shaved except for a lock of hair just above the neck. The boy kept that lock until he entered his first battle and brought back at least one prisoner. Taking an enemy soldier prisoner was more important than killing him because prisoners were sacrificed to the gods. Battle-hardened soldiers who had captured many foes were invited to join heroic orders within the military, such as the Jaguar Order and the Eagle Order. Elaborate laws allowed members of the special orders to wear headdresses made of bright feathers and permitted them to march in honored spots during army parades.

Courage in battle was expected of all Aztec men. To display cowardice in any form was an unthinkable disgrace. Retreating in the face of an enemy was a crime that called for the death penalty, but almost never did that punishment have to be imposed. A typical Aztec soldier buried his fear of death deep in his thoughts and fought in battle with a fury that shocked his foes. Since the boy's childhood, teachers, priests, parents, and relatives drummed it into his head that he had sacred duty to uphold. He lived only to defend and expand his nation. Poems told him that the battlefield was a thrilling place, a theater of high adventure:

> The battlefield is the place
> where one toasts the divine liquor in war,
> where are stained red the divine eagles,
> where the jaguars howl,
> where all kinds of precious stones rain from the ornaments,
> where wave headdresses rich with fine plumes,
> where princes are smashed to bits.

Women were not directly involved in the military. Girls were taught singing and dancing, but they did not attend a formal school. Few girls learned to read and write. Young, unmarried girls were expected to walk with their heads down and attract no attention. Weaving cotton clothes was a required task for all females. Women often ran small stands in the markets, and they were known to be shrewd bargainers. However, in matters of the state and the military, women were second-class citizens in Aztec society.

Aztec males married at about age twenty, and girls at fourteen or fifteen. Parents arranged a daughter's marriage with the help of a fortune-teller who paid close attention to the birth dates of the girl and the groom-to-be. A marriage ceremony was celebrated by a great feast, usually paid for by the bride's family. Parents of the bride hoped their son-in-law would prove to be a kindly and responsible young man. No laws protected a woman who had the bad fortune to have an abusive husband.

Slavery was an accepted institution among the Aztecs. No one was born a slave in Aztec society. A judge could sentence a man or a woman into slavery after he or she committed repeated crimes. Often a man, who through bad luck or laziness could not feed his family, offered himself for sale as a slave, and the goods or money earned from the sale went to support his wife and children. Slaves were treated with a degree of respect, but an enslaved person had no rights. They were bought and sold in the markets as if they were turkeys. If an owner wished to donate a slave to the priests to be sacrificed, the slave was dispatched and had no say in the matter.

Aztec law allowed slaves a curious escape clause. If a slave who was waiting to be sold at the Tenochtitlán market bolted and ran as far as the emperor's palace, a distance of a little more than a mile, the slave was granted freedom. The law said that only the owner or the owner's son was allowed to chase the runaway. Anyone else who chased and caught the escapee was himself sentenced to slavery.

The Aztecs valued an orderly society and expected all their citizens to abide by its rules. Lawbreakers received harsh punishments. Public drunkenness was condemned as ugly behavior. A man who was judged drunk had his head shaved and his house knocked down for the first offense. A second offense of drunkenness merited the death penalty. Adultery was also thought of as a criminal act. A man caught cheating on his wife was stoned to death; his body was left to be eaten by buzzards.

Life after death was a complicated concept for the Aztecs. Hell had nine levels and heaven thirteen. The deceased person had to forge blindly through this maze of heavens and hells to discover the level that suited him. Moreover, it was not the quality of one's life that determined his or her place in the next world; it was instead the manner of one's death. A warrior dying on the battlefield was instantly propelled to the highest place in heaven. A woman dying in childbirth was also rewarded with an eternity of pleasure and happiness. Sacrificial victims became "companions to the eagle" and soared into the sky after enduring the ordeal of death at the altar. Simply dying of old age in one's house meant an uncertain and possibly an unexciting or even painful afterlife.

A welcome break in the Aztec routine of work and worship came during festival times. Calendars were carefully marked, noting the dates and the nature of upcoming festivals. Some festivals were solemn and religious in nature, and they included human sacrifice. Other grand, nationwide parties were devoted to pure joy. During the revelry, flutes made of hollowed-out bones shrilled and drums sounded. Men and women danced to the music, and bright feathers decorated homes. Festivals could last as many as ten days and nights. During one particularly wild festival, men tied ropes to their ankles and dangled upside down as the ropes slowly unwound from a thick pole. This flying act from a pole is still practiced in Mexico. The male participants are called *Los Voladores*, The Flyers.

The Aztecs built their mighty empire based on two characteristics of their people: discipline and fatalism. Discipline was an accepted way of life. When a superior gave an order, it was carried out without question, even if it meant death to the person exercising the order. A belief in fatalism rendered death tolerable, perhaps even desirable, in the Aztec mind. An Aztec citizen was born to die. To go to great lengths to avoid death was useless because it meant fighting the forces of nature itself. The inevitability and acceptance of death is seen in this favorite Aztec poem:

Los Voladores, the Flyers, perform a ceremonial ritual as a part of the festivities still practiced today in Mexico.

We only came to sleep
we only came to dream;
it is not true, no it is not true
that we came to live on this earth.

This disciplined society, led by fearless soldiers, carved out the Aztec Empire. That huge empire was not like a European country, where all subjects lived under the rule of one king. Instead, the Aztec nation was a collection of more or less independent city-states whose leaders agreed to pay tributes to Tenochtitlán. Tributes, paid as if they were taxes, included gold, bales of cotton, deerskins, and slaves. All of these goods were sent to Tenochtitlán, where they made the rich city even richer. The most precious commodity sent to the capital were men and women slated to be slaughtered on Aztec altars.

The Aztecs admired the Toltecs to the point of hero-worship. A talented painter was said to "paint like a Toltec," or a gifted sculptor "carved like a Toltec." The Toltecs were prodigious in putting people to death on their altars. In this area too the Aztecs followed the older culture's lead. But no society in Mesoamerican history, or perhaps even in the history of the world, was as devoted to human sacrifice as were the Aztecs. In the years when the Aztecs were desert wanderers, human sacrifice was an occasional ritual performed by their priests. The Hummingbird was then their god of the hunt, and from time to time he needed the death of human beings if he were to bless the mission of tribal hunters. When the Aztecs became empire-builders, the Hummingbird rose in status to become the god of war. Now, as the lord of battle, the Hummingbird had to be given human blood or he would condemn the nation's mighty army to certain defeat on the battlefield. Other gods—the rain god, the wind god, the fire god, the god who protected crops—demanded human hearts. In the 1500s, as the society reached its greatest heights, thousands of people were killed every year at the altars of the Aztec Empire.

A warrior's heart was strong, and upon death he imparted that strength to the gods. Therefore, so the Aztecs reasoned, prisoners of war were the most desirable sacrificial victims. Rival cultures entertained similar beliefs. Often the Aztec army fought "flower wars" with other city-states. The object of the arranged battles was to gather captives. In addition to war prisoners, slaves were frequent sacrificial victims. A rich Aztec man gained special blessings by donating slaves to the priests for use at the altars. Women were sacrificed, but not as frequently as were men.

Sadly, children too met their deaths at the altars. The rain god Tlaloc, always important in drought-strickened central Mexico, hungered for children. A priest serving the cult of Tlaloc could simply approach a family, point to a child, and lead him or her off to the altars. Parents grieved when one of their children was selected to die for the rain god. The children were terrified to be taken to their deaths, but the general public seemed to approve of the practice of offering the lives of young people to a deity. An Aztec wrote, "And when the priests took the children to the places where they would be killed, if they cried and shed many tears, the onlookers became joyful because [the tears were] considered a sign that the rains would come soon."

The hearts of sacrificial victims were stuffed in a bowl especially designed to hold the organs. The remains of the body were butchered, cooked, and eaten. Only the upper classes, high-ranking army officers, and priests were permitted to eat human flesh. Cooks, following written recipes, prepared special dishes for the privileged few—human meat stewed with corn, human meat cooked with chili peppers.

Mysticism, magic, and the awesome power of the gods ruled Aztec thinking. The people saw war and strife everywhere. The rainy season did not simply arrive in the early summer months; instead, the angels commanded by the rain god waged war against the devils of drought. Cosmic wars were fought ceaselessly between good and evil. There was no way to stop the endless battles. The gods needed strength to bring fortune to the Aztec people. Hence, the gods required human blood and hearts. To deny the gods their rightful needs would serve only to usher in the end of the universe.

An Aztec human sacrifice as depicted in the *Historia de las Indias* by Diego Duran published in Madrid in 1579

Neu Mexiko,

249

An artist's impression of the deity
Quetzalcoatl, the Feathered Serpent

CHAPTER 9

The Feathered Serpent Returns

Birth, life, death—to the Aztecs this was the inevitable pattern, not only for individual men and women but for the universe as well. According to the Aztec Legend of the Suns, the universe had already been created and destroyed four times. Each time-cycle was called a Sun. The Aztecs believed they lived during the period of the Fifth Sun, and that Sun too would eventually die. How and when the Fifth Sun would die was unknown, but destruction was a certainty because it was the will of the gods. The always-fatalistic Aztecs waited for the death of the Fifth Sun and tried to placate the gods as they waited.

Pleasing the gods meant sending victims to their altars. As long as the gods were placated with blood and human hearts, they would aid the Aztec nation and delay the death of the Fifth Sun. But one god was an enigma and therefore very difficult to please. He was Quetzalcoatl, the Feathered Serpent.

The Aztecs freely borrowed religious ideas and gods from other cultures. Quetzalcoatl came from the people they admired the most: the Toltecs. The Feathered Serpent was worshiped by many cultures in ancient Mexico, but among the Toltecs he was both a god and a living, breathing ruler. Hundreds of years ago, the serpent called Quetzalcoatl lived among the Toltecs and acted as a king and as a teacher in their society. It was said that he taught the Toltecs new farming techniques and instructed them in metalworking.

Unique among Mexico's gods, he alone condemned human sacrifice. The Feathered Serpent shunned bloody hearts, preferring instead to accept gifts of flowers and butterflies. This rejection of human sacrifice hinted at Quetzalcoatl having a gentle nature, but the Aztecs could not forget his angry and vengeful side. Generations earlier, the Feathered Serpent had been driven away by a rival god. Before he went into exile, the Serpent vowed to return and claim all of Mexico as his realm. Priests and scholars knew that Quetzalcoatl had predicted that he would return in 1519. That year, the year One Reed on the Aztec calendar, coincided with the height of Aztec power. By 1519, the Aztec Empire had grown to be so mighty that it seemed no one—not even a god—could topple its structure.

Was Quetzalcoatl of the Toltecs a European?

In the 1000s, the Vikings left the Scandinavian countries to sail across the Atlantic to Iceland, Greenland, and even North America. Irish monks, seeking solitude so they could meditate, also took long ocean voyages and settled in remote spots. Could a monk or a Viking explorer have entered Mexico some one thousand years ago? Certainly, a Christian person would have preached against human sacrifice, as did Quetzalcoatl of old. In Aztec paintings, Quetzalcoatl was often pictured as a white man with a beard—unusual facial features in ancient Mexico. Theories abound that the Feathered Serpent was a European, perhaps a Christian priest, who washed up on Mexican shores in ancient times and was worshiped as a god.

Heading the Aztec nation in 1519 was Emperor Montezuma II. In his youth, he had been a warrior who led soldiers into many victories on the battlefield. According to tradition, all Aztec rulers had to come from a military background. Montezuma was named emperor in 1502 and now, at about age forty, he assumed he was the most powerful man in the world. His was the greatest empire in Mesoamerican history. Its capital, Tenochtitlán, was a dream city composed of canals, arrow-straight streets, castles, and lofty pyramids. An Aztec poet pondered this invincible empire and its shining capital city and wrote:

> Who could conquer Tenochtitlán?
> Who could shake the foundation of heaven. . . .

As was true with all Aztecs, Emperor Montezuma believed that mystical signs in the sky and elsewhere heralded great events to come. In 1519, unexplainable incidents were observed everywhere in his empire. A bright three-headed comet, "like a fiery fuse, like a flame," hung in the sky night after night. Aztec astronomers were unable to explain the significance of this mysterious comet. A woman was said to haunt the streets of the capital during the late evenings, wailing to unseen sons: "O my beloved sons, we are all going to die." Reports from a general claimed that an Aztec army was driven out of a distant province by rocks that rained down from the sky.

Most disturbing to Montezuma was the sudden presence of "wooden houses" seen on the Atlantic Ocean to the south and east of his empire. They were boats that were said to be gigantic. They held many sailors and had "clouds" above their decks. The men on board the vessels were foreign, even alien-looking. An Aztec army officer reported to Montezuma, "It is true that there have come to the shore I do not know what kind of people. Some of them were fishing there with rods. . . . Then they got into a canoe and went back to the thing on the sea with two towers and went into it. . . . The skins of these people are white, much more than our skins are. All of them have long beards and hair down to their ears."

Artists depicted Quetzalcoatl as a white man with a beard. Generations earlier, the serpent deity had warned he would return in the year One Reed and come back over the Atlantic Ocean. Now strange white men appeared on the coast at the same time and same place where the Feathered Serpent had claimed he would reappear. Were the men on these huge boats gods commanded by Quetzalcoatl himself? If so, Montezuma and his priests asked the ultimate question: will the serpent deity, now that he has returned, order the dreaded end times—the death of the Fifth Sun?

Some 4,000 miles across the Atlantic lay the Kingdom of Spain. Like the Aztec nation, it was a militaristic society, and its people lived in fear of divine forces. Unlike the Aztecs, the Spaniards believed in one God, the Christian God. Both the Spaniards and the Aztecs believed their supreme being (or beings) were all-powerful and must be obeyed at all times. The arrival of the Spaniards in Mexico triggered a bloody war pitting the Christian God against their gods.

Christopher Columbus's voyage in 1492 opened the door of the Americas to Europeans. Spaniards were first to take advantage of this opening. In the early 1500s, Spanish colonists built settlements on islands in the Caribbean Sea: Cuba, Puerto Rico, and Hispaniola (today Haiti and the Dominican Republic). Those Spaniards were the conquistadors (conquerors). They were ruthless fighters who quickly overwhelmed the primitive people that they encountered on the Caribbean islands.

The Spaniards had hoped that by sailing west they could reach the rich nations of China and India. Instead they landed on the Caribbean Islands, and they were disappointed. They had sought gold and spices and found little of either. Moreover, their new territory consisted of relatively small islands. They had scant idea that the huge landmass of Mexico lay to their west.

An engraving of Spanish conquistadors
receiving gifts from Native Americans while
soldiers raise a Christian cross in the background

The conquistadors enslaved the Caribbean people, extracted from them what little gold they found, and forced them to follow the teachings of their God. The men from Spain were military adventurers who believed in Christianizing others by the sword if necessary. Historians have summed up their mission in the New World in three words: God, gold, glory.

The most aggressive of the conquistadors was Hernán Cortés, born in 1485 to a family that had little wealth but enjoyed a noble standing. Cortés came to Cuba at a young age and acquired slaves and land. Always ambitious, he clashed with the Spanish governor of Cuba but still managed to gather a fleet of ships and a small army. Cortés wished to investigate reports made by other Spanish sailors that a new land lay to the west. The men claimed that as they sailed along the shores of this new land, they saw cities with tall pyramids. What they saw were actually the ruins of old Mayan pyramids, but in the Spanish imagination they loomed as affluent urban dwellings. Spain had long been haunted by stories that a wealthy civilization stood across the Atlantic. Tales said it was a place so rich that even the peasants there ate from solid gold plates.

In 1519, Cortés and his army of 550 soldiers and sixteen horses landed at what is now the city of Veracruz, Mexico. He fought with the natives and quickly subdued them thanks to his horses and firearms. He then asked the coastal people if they had gold. They showed him a few pieces. Cortés inquired where he could find more. The people pointed to the mountains to the west and said, "Mexico, Mexico." Coastal dwellers called the Aztecs the *Mexica*; their great capital city, Tenochtitlán, was called Mexico.

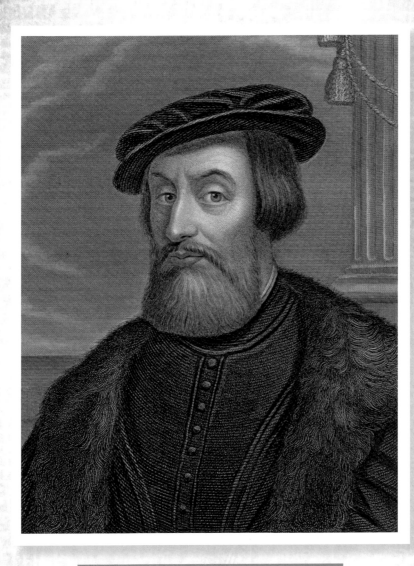

An 1833 engraving of Hernán Cortés, by
William Holl the Younger of England.

Horses in the New World

All Native Americans were shocked when they saw the Spaniards riding their marvelous horses. People in the Americas called them deer because deer were the only animals they knew of that even resembled these beasts. But unlike deer, these animals seemed almost human. The native people saw the Spaniards talk to their horses, telling them to stop or turn, and they believed the horses were able to talk back. Many ancient Mexicans thought the horse and the rider were one creature. In an early encounter with a conquistador army, the Mexicans saw a man fall off his horse and quickly remount. The accidental fall stunned the Mexican soldiers. This godlike creature could divide itself into two and rejoin again at its will.

Through an incredible network of runners, Montezuma was kept informed about Cortés's activities on the Atlantic coast. Relay teams of specially trained runners passed messages over the mountainous 250-mile path from the coast to the capital in just twenty-four hours. Through the messages, Montezuma learned that these men rode on the backs of enormous "deer." They owned "firesticks" that sounded like thunder and could kill a foe from a distance. They spoke of a new god, and they told the coastal people that human sacrifice was sinful. The conclusion was clear: these men who came from the sea were gods, and their leader was Quetzalcoatl himself.

Cortés and his followers began a trek over the mountains toward Tenochtitlán. The Spanish mission was bold. A military clash would pit Cortés's few hundred men against the entire Aztec army, a force that had never tasted defeat in its history. One of the Spanish soldiers, Bernal Díaz del Castillo, mused about the brave, even foolishly brave conquistadors and wrote, "Let the curious readers consider whether there is not much to ponder over in this that I am writing. What men have there been in the world who have shown such daring?"

Díaz del Castillo's Story of the Conquest

Bernal Díaz del Castillo was a soldier in Cortés's army and an eyewitness to the Spanish conquest of Mexico. About fifty years after the conquest, the elderly Díaz del Castillo wrote *The Discovery and Conquest of Mexico*. It is a fine source book and an excellent read. The author was privileged to see the Aztec society in all its glory. Moreover, the book was written from the point of view of a man who admired the Aztecs and their many accomplishments.

To dash any second thoughts his men might harbor about retreating from a confrontation with the mighty Aztec army, Cortés ordered his fleet of ships to be burned. Now, with his vessels reduced to hulks, there could be no turning back for the Spanish soldiers. They must follow their chief even into death. Commander Cortés was able to talk to the people of the Veracruz region through two interpreters. One was Malinche, a slave woman, who spoke both the Mayan tongue and Nahuatl. The other was Gerónimo de Aguilar, a Spanish sailor who had been shipwrecked in Mexico ten years earlier. He lived among the Maya and had learned their language. With the aid of this translator team, Cortés befriended a coastal leader whom he called the "Fat Chief." The hefty king told him that the Aztecs were cruel overlords who forced their vassal city-states to pay too much in tributes. If Cortés wished to conquer Tenochtitlán, the Fat Chief claimed, his soldiers would be happy to assist him.

As Cortés approached the capital, Montezuma tried, with cunning and force, to turn the Spanish army away. He sent emissaries bearing gifts of gold, but the presents only whetted the Spanish appetite for even more of the precious metal. Cortés told one Aztec agent, "I and my companions suffer from a disease of the heart which can be cured only by gold." At Cholula, Montezuma ordered the Aztec army to attack the foreigners. However, the slave woman Malinche learned of

the intended assault the night before and informed Cortés. In the en-
suing battle, the conquistadors slaughtered the Aztecs. After Cholula,
Emperor Montezuma gave up trying to stop the Spaniards' march and
grimly accepted his fate. He reasoned that Cortés was a god, and not
even the powerful chief of the Aztec nation could possibly challenge
the will of a deity.

In November 1519, the Spaniards saw the outskirts of the city of
Tenochtitlán. They were wonderstruck. Never had they imagined that
such a rich and beautiful city existed anywhere in the world. Bernal
Díaz del Castillo wrote, "we were amazed [as we entered the city for
the first time] and said it was like the enchantments they tell us in the
legend[s] . . . on account of the great towers and cues and buildings
rising from the water. . . . And some of the soldiers even wondered
whether the things we saw [about us] were not a dream."

Montezuma and Cortés greeted each other with the dignity such
an occasion warranted. The two men exchanged gifts. Cortés gave

A sixteenth-century illustration of the meeting of Cortés and Montezuma from the *History of the Indies* by Diego Duran

Montezuma a necklace studded with pearls, and the Aztec leader presented the Spaniard with a band containing gold figures of shrimp, all delicately carved. They shook hands. Cortés began to give Montezuma the traditional Spanish *abrazo* (hug), but he was stopped by Montezuma's aides. In Aztec society, no one was permitted to look directly at the emperor, much less hug or even touch him. The meeting was truly unique in history. Here were the leaders of two advanced cultures that had developed on opposite sides of the world. Just a few months earlier, one society had not even dreamed of the existence of the other. Now, finally, the leaders had come together.

The Spaniards were treated as honored guests. They were housed in a castle that once belonged to Montezuma's father. Servants brought them the best food available in the capital city. Even the horses were offered turkey dinners.

After the Spaniards rested, Aztec officials took them on a tour of the capital. The foreigners saw the city's great open market, where

123

goods were arranged with vegetables in one section, grains in another, and honey in still another. Most of the soldiers had visited cities in Europe, but never had they seen a marketplace so clean and orderly as this. They entered Montezuma's private zoo. Díaz del Castillo wrote that "the jackals and foxes howled and the serpents hissed, it was horrible to listen to and it sounded like hell."

Nothing prepared the Spaniards for their tour of the temple on top of the city's tallest pyramid. This was the holiest spot in the empire, the place where human sacrifices were performed. At the entrance stood the statue of Huitzilopochtli, which Díaz del Castillo claimed had "a very broad face and monstrous and terrible eyes." Deeper inside they saw the hearts of men who had been sacrificed just hours earlier. The scene sickened the conquistadors. Díaz del Castillo wrote: "All the walls of the [temple] were so splashed and encrusted with blood that they were black . . . the whole place stank vilely."

Human Sacrifice and the Spaniards

The Spaniards regarded human sacrifice as a horrible practice, one that demonstrated the inferiority of the Aztec religion. But in their own society, the conquistadors had seen men and women put to death in a most cruel manner, also in the name of God. The Inquisition, a time of religious excess, held sway in Spain and much of Europe during the 1500s. Inquisition priests accused people of heresy and had them burned at the stake in macabre ceremonies watched by hundreds. The agony of the victims was never-ending. Priests claimed that those burned at the stake suffered even after death because the crime of heresy was punished by an eternity of hell's fires. Aztec sacrificial victims, on the other hand, were told that their souls would ascend into the heavens after their ordeal on the altars.

The Spaniards were shaken by their visit to the temple, but they kept civil relations with the Aztecs. Then, six days into the visit, Cortés made his boldest move. He seized Montezuma and put him in chains. The Aztec emperor and his guards were too shocked to resist. The people did not rise up against this outrage because no one ordered them to do so. Ironclad discipline was the Aztec strength, but it was also the society's most glaring weakness. The Aztecs would willingly fight until death if their emperor so ordered. However, now that their emperor was a prisoner, they were stupefied into inaction. They had no leader to follow.

For more than six months, Montezuma was held a captive in his own palace. Life continued at a normal pace in the capital, which Cortés now ruled. But gradually the Aztec people realized that the outsiders were not gods, as they had once thought. In May 1520, Spaniards and Aztecs fought near the city's tallest pyramid. On June 30, 1520, the Aztecs rose up and, after a ferocious battle, drove the Spaniards out of their city. Forever after, the night of June 30 was called *La Noche Triste* (The Sad Night) in Mexican history because so many Aztecs and Spaniards lost their lives in the fighting.

The Sad Night marked the start of a war between the conquistadors and the Aztec nation. The war lasted more than a year, and during the course of battle the magnificent city of Tenochtitlán was completely destroyed. The Aztec Empire also dissolved under Spanish might. For the Aztecs, the Death of the Fifth Sun was now a reality. An Aztec poet lamented,

> Broken spears lie in the roads
> The houses are roofless . . .
> Weep, weep, our people.
> For we have lost Mexico.

An artist's impression of the Aztecs' attack on the Spanish invaders in Tenochtitlan during La Noche Triste in 1520

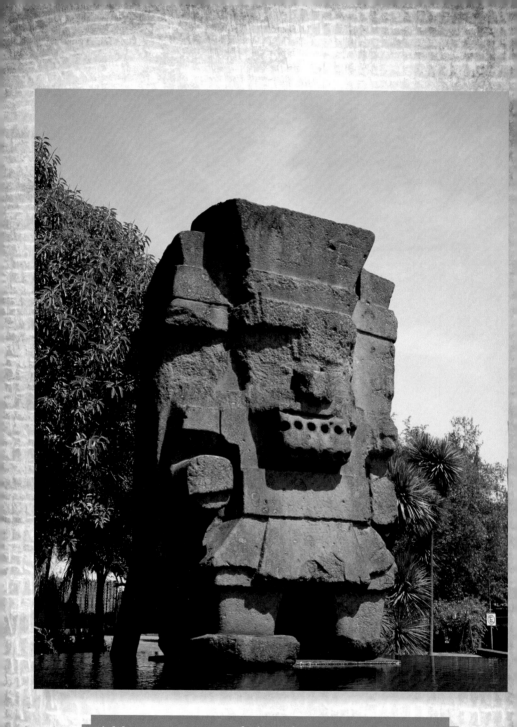

A Mayan stone statue of a head from Coatlinchan outside
the National Museum of Anthropology in Mexico City

CHAPTER 10

The Legacy of Ancient Mexico

In a Mexico City neighborhood not far from the heart of the metropolis is a public square called La Plaza de Tres Culturas (The Plaza of Three Cultures). The square contains the ruins of an Aztec temple, a Spanish church built in the 1500s, and a modern glass and concrete apartment complex. These buildings within the plaza represent the three eras that shaped Mexico: the ancient period, the Spanish era, and modern times. Mexican schools teach students their country's history separated into these three chapters. Every day, groups of schoolchildren come to the plaza led by teachers who explain the significance of the structures and the time periods they represent. Nowhere else in Mexico do the three chapters of the country's history come together so neatly as they do in La Plaza de Tres Culturas.

The Spanish era began immediately after Cortés conquered the Aztecs in 1521. Spanish colonists flocked to the country that Cortés renamed New Spain. The Spaniards called New Spain's capital Mexico City, after the word the coastal people used. A new city rose on the ruins of the old. Often the churches and homes of Spanish Mexico City were built with bricks taken from demolished Aztec pyramids.

The Ghosts of Tenochtitlán

Mexico City rose over the ruins of Tenochtitlán. The ancient city lay below the streets of the new capital as if it were entombed. Now and then, the ghosts of the past were unearthed. In 1790, workers digging a basement for a new building in the center of the city uncovered a twenty-six-ton disc that was once the Aztec Calendar Stone. The great disc now is displayed in Mexico City's National Museum of Anthropology. In the 1970s, crews digging a trench for an electrical cable discovered a buried temple complex. The complex was carefully preserved and is now Templo Mayor (Main Temple), an outdoor museum in the great plaza called the Zocalo. Undoubtedly, more ghosts of Tenochtitlán lie below the modern metropolis, awaiting discovery.

From the capital, the Spaniards spread out, establishing gold mines and large farms in the provinces. Mexico became the richest colony in the vast Spanish Empire. In the process of expansion, the Europeans made virtual slaves out of the native people. Spain introduced the Christian religion and the Spanish language to Mexico. The Spanish era lasted three hundred years, until 1821, when the Mexican people rose up to win their independence.

Under Spain a new race, the mestizo race, was born. Mestizos are mixed-race people, a product of the union between white Europeans (mostly Spaniards) and darker Indian people. At first mestizos were a minority, but the race grew rapidly. Today, about nine out of ten Mexicans call themselves mestizos. Often the word *mestizo* is omitted and mixed race people are simply referred to as *La Raza*, The Race. Columbus Day, a national holiday held in October, is called *Dia de la Raza* (Day of the Race) to honor Christopher Columbus, whose 1492 voyage led to the creation of the mestizo race.

Of Mexico's three historic periods, the ancient or Pre-Columbian was by far the longest. From the Olmecs to the Aztecs, ancient Mexico lasted more than 2,000 years. Mexicans see their Pre-Columbian era as a golden age as well as a frightening time in their past. Certainly ancient Mexico—from the brilliance of the Maya to the blood and splendor of the Aztecs—shaped the modern nation and its people. Octavio Paz, a Mexican philosopher and Nobel Prize winner, wrote, "The history of Mexico is a history of a man seeking his parentage, his origins. He wants to go back beyond the catastrophe he suffered, he wants to be the sun again."

TIMELINE

15,000 YEARS AGO

The first human beings enter North America (many scholars believe they came thousands of years earlier).

10,000 YEARS AGO

Ancient peoples arrive in what is now Mexico (again, numerous authorities think they arrived much earlier).

6000 TO 4000 BCE

Ancient people in Mexico begin to cultivate corn, and the practice spreads throughout the Americas.

2000 BCE

Pottery and sculpture flourish in Mexico.

1500 BCE

Zapotec farmers begin cultivating fields in what is today the state of Oaxaca.

1200 BCE

The Olmec culture in the Gulf of Mexico region begins.

1100 BCE

Pyramids are built at the Olmec religious center of La Venta.

1000 BCE

The Mayan society develops in southern Mexico and Guatemala.

750 BCE

Workers construct the Purron Dam, Mexico's first large water conservation project.

500 BCE

Work starts on the ambitious project of flattening the peak of Monte Albán in order to build a religious center there.

400 BCE

For unknown reasons, the Olmecs, Mexico's "mother culture," declines.

400 BCE

The city of Cholula is founded.

50 BCE

A volcanic eruption buries the Pyramid of Cuicuilco and destroys the religious center there.

150 CE

Work begins on the planned city of Teotihuacán.

700

Teotihuacán is destroyed, perhaps at the hands of an outside army or because of an internal uprising.

700

Mayan civilization declines rapidly.

700

Human sacrifice and warfare between city-states increase throughout ancient Mexico.

750

The Zapotec culture declines and is replaced by the Mixtec people in Oaxaca.

900

The Toltecs rise in the Valley of Mexico.

1200

Toltec civilization fades.

1325

A wandering Aztec tribe claims to see the miraculous vision of an eagle perched on a cactus while eating a snake.

1400s

The Aztec build the great city of Tenochtitlán in the Valley of Mexico.

C. 1480

Montezuma, the future emperor of the Aztec nation, is born.

1485

Hernán Cortés is born in Spain.

1492

Italian sea captain Christopher Columbus, sailing on a mission for Spain, lands on islands in the Caribbean Sea.

1502

Montezuma is named emperor of the Aztecs.

1504

Cortés leaves Spain and settles in the Caribbean region.

1519

Leading a small Spanish fleet, Cortés lands on Mexican soil near present-day Veracruz; at first, the Mexican people believe he is a returning god.

1521

After a war lasting many months, the Spaniards defeat the Aztecs, ending Mexico's ancient (Pre-Columbian) historical period.

SOURCES

CHAPTER ONE: **The Land and Its First Inhabitants**
p. 15,   "In all the New World . . ." Michael Coe, *Mexico: From the Olmecs to the Aztecs* (New York: Thames & Hudson Inc., 1994), 23.

CHAPTER TWO: **The Olmecs**
p. 25,   "in a certain . . ." Coe, *Mexico*, 61.
p. 31,   "The Olmecs were not only . . ." Karl E. Meyer, *Teotihuacán: First City in the Americas* (New York: Newsweek Press, 1978), 38.
p. 31,   "The stone was so transparent . . ." Karl Ernest Meyers, *Teotihuacan: Wonders of Man* (New York: *Newsweek*, 1973), 42.
p. 32,   "one can imagine . . ." Coe, *Mexico*, 75.
p. 32,   "was destroyed by . . ." Ibid., 69.
p. 34,   "Civilizations went out with a . . ." Ibid., 70.

CHAPTER THREE: **The Mystery People and Their Mystery City**
p. 40,   "Even though it was night . . ." Coe, *Mexico*, 94.
p. 50,   "And they called it . . ." Ibid., 102-103.

CHAPTER FOUR: **Time and the Maya**
p. 54,   "As much as 85 percent . . ." Michael Coe, *The Maya* (New York: Thames and Hudson, 1993), 190.
p. 54,   "We found a great number . . ." Tony Allan and Tom Lowenstein, *Gods of Sun and Sacrifice* (London: Duncan Baird Publishing, 1997), 143.
p. 55,   "A high civilization had no business . . ." *National Geographic Magazine*, August 2007.
p. 62,   "I conceive the endless . . ." Ronald Wright, *Time Among the Maya* (New York: Grove Press, 2000), 94.

CHAPTER SIX: **Mexico in the Classic Period**
p. 80,   "Above all, the inhabitants . . ." Coe, *Mexico*, 118.
p. 83,   "full of skulls . . ." Bernal Díaz del Castillo, *The Discovery and Conquest of Mexico* (New York: Da Capo Press, 1996), 123.

CHAPTER SEVEN: **The Toltecs: Warrior/Poets**
p. 89,   "A battle-scarred, militaristic . . ." Thomas H. Flaherty, ed., *Aztecs: Reign of Blood & Splendor* (Alexandria, Va.: Time-Life Books, 1992), 65.
p. 93,   "Everywhere there meets the eye . . ." Coe, *Mexico*, 134.

CHAPTER EIGHT: **The Rise of the Aztecs**
p. 95,   "There [the Aztecs] feasted . . ." Jonathan Kandell, *La Capital: The Biography of Mexico City* (New York: Random House, 1988), 26.
p. 96,   "[L]ater, when they left . . ." Ibid., 26.
p. 97,   "And when the [Aztecs] arrived . . ." Ibid., 27.

p. 100,   "The city is spread out . . ." Jon Manchip White, *Cortés and the Downfall of the Aztec Empire* (New York: Carroll & Graf Publishers, 1971), 99.
p. 102,   "The main goal . . ." Coe, *Mexico*, 175.
p. 104,   "The battlefield is the place . . ." Ibid., 176.
p. 108,   "We only came to sleep . . ." Hugh Thomas, *Conquest: Montezuma, Cortés, and the Fall of Old Mexico* (New York: Simon & Schuster, 1993), 309.
p. 109,   "And when the priests . . ." Kandell, *La Capital*, 60.

CHAPTER NINE: The Feahered Serpent Returns
p. 115,   "Who could conquer . . ." Thomas, *Conquest*, 5.
p. 115,   "like a fiery fuse . . ." Kandell, 68.
p. 115,   "O my beloved sons . . ." Ibid.
p. 115,   "It is true that there . . ." Thomas, *Conquest*, 48.
p. 120,   "Let the curious readers . . ." Díaz del Castillo, *The Discovery and Conquest of Mexico*, 192.
p. 121,   "I and my companions . . ." Kandell, *La Capital*, 98.
p. 122,   "we were amazed . . ." Bernal Diaz del Castillo, *The Discovery and Conquest of Mexico* (Cambridge, MA Da Capo Press, 2003), 190.
p. 124,   "the jackals and foxes . . ." Ibid., 213.
p. 124,   "All the walls of the [temple] . . ." Ibid., 219-220.
p. 125,   "Broken spears lie in the roads . . ." T. R. Fehrenbach, *Fire and Blood: A History of Mexico* (New York: Macmillan, 1973), 146.

CHAPTER TEN: The Legacy of Ancient Mexico
p. 131,   "The history of Mexico . . ." Octavio Paz, *The Labyrinth of Solitude* (New York: Grove Press, 1985), 20.

BIBLIOGRAPHY

Allan, Tony, and Tom Lowenstein. *Gods of Sun and Sacrifice*. London: Duncan Baird Publishing, 1997.

Coe, Michael. *Mexico: From the Olmecs to the Aztecs*. New York: Thames & Hudson, Inc., 1994.

_____. *The Maya*. New York: Thames & Hudson, Inc., 1993.

Davies, Nigel. *The Ancient Kingdoms of Mexico*. London: Penguin Books, 1982.

Díaz del Castillo, Bernal. *The Discovery and Conquest of Mexico*. New York: Da Capo Press, 1996.

Fehrenbach, T. R. *Fire and Blood: A History of Mexico*. New York: Macmillan, 1973.

Flaherty, Thomas H., ed. *Aztecs: Reign of Blood & Splendor*. Alexandria, Va.: Time-Life Books, 1992.

Kandell, Jonathan. *La Capital: The Biography of Mexico City*. New York: Random House, 1988.

Leon-Portilla, Miguel, ed. *Broken Spears: The Aztec Account of the Conquest of Mexico*. Boston: Beacon Press, 1992.

Markman, Roberta H., and Peter T. Markman. *The Flayed God: The Mesoamerican Mythological Tradition*. New York: HarperCollins, 1992.

McKillop, Heather. *The Ancient Maya: New Perspectives*. New York: W. W. Norton & Company, 2004.

Meyer, Karl E. *Teotihuacán: First City in the Americas*. New York: Newsweek Press, 1978.

Paz, Octavio. *The Labyrinth of Solitude*. New York: Grove Press, 1985.

Ruiz, Eduardo. *Triumphs and Tragedy: A History of the Mexican People*. New York: W. W. Norton & Company, 1992.

Thomas, Hugh. *Conquest: Montezuma, Cortés, and the Fall of Old Mexico*. New York: Simon & Schuster, 1993.

White, Jon Manchip. *Cortés and the Downfall of the Aztec Empire*. New York: Carroll & Graf Publishers, 1971.

Wright, Ronald. *Time Among the Maya*. New York: Grove Press, 2000.

de Zorita, Alonzo. *Life and Labor in Ancient Mexico*. New Brunswick, N.J.: Rutgers University Press, 1971.

WEB SITES

http://www.ancientmexico.com

Profiles the Aztecs, Toltecs, Maya, Olmecs, and other peoples of Mesoamerica.

http://www.mexicocity.com.mx/anc_city.html

Offers a nice synopsis about Tenochtitlán, up through 1522.

http://www.geographia.com/mexico/mexicohistory.htm

Provides an overview of Mexico's history, up to modern times.

INDEX

Ancient Mexico
  and agriculture, 38
  archelogical finds, 22, 42, 68
  Archaic Period, 78
  arts and crafts, 79
  cities of, 79-80
  Classic Period, 43, 55, 77-80,
    82-83
  culture of, 77
  decline of, 82-83
  geography, 12, 14-16, 38, 82-83
  legacy of, 129-131
  myths, 12
  Postclassic Period, 78
  Preclassic Period, 78
  and pyramids, 80
  rituals, 83
  social life and customs, 79-80,
    82-83
atlatl (spear), 14
Atzlan, 95-96
Avenue of the Dead, 41-43, *44-45*
Aztec Indians, 37-38, 41, 78-79,
  85-86, 89, 93, 131
  and agriculture, 17, 100, 102
  and calendars, 114
  culture of, 96-99, 105, 124
  engineering skills, 99-100, 102
  legends and folklore, 40, 95-97,
    113-116, 120
  military strengths, 95, 97, 99,
    102-104, 109
  power as an empire, 114-115
  and pyramids, 118
  religious practices, 40-41, 98, 106,
    108-109, 114, 116
  rituals, 23, *110-111*, 113-114, 124
  settlement in Tenochtitlán, 97-99

social life and customs, 100,
    103-106, 108
  Spanish conquest of, 116, 121-125

calendars, 42, *52*, 55, 62, 78, 92,
  106, 114, 130, *130*
Calendar Stone, 130, *130*
Calmecacs (schools), 103
Cascajal Block, 27, *27*
Central Plateau, 12, 14, 16, 19, 49
chacmools (statues), *84*, 88
Chapultepec, 102
Chíchen Itzá (city), 59, *60-61*, 80,
  87-88
Chichimeca nomads, 82-83, 85
chinampas (farms), 100, 102
Cholula (city), 46, 79, 82, 89,
  121-122
Clovis Point Spears, 11, *11*
Cocijo (god), 22, 71
codices (books), 54, 63, 73
Colhuacan (state), 97
Columbus, Christopher, 78, 116,
  131
Cortés, Hernán, 14, 118, *119*,
  120-123, *122-123*, 125, 129
Cuicuilco Pyramid, 38-40, *39*

Danzantes (Dancers) (stone relief),
  69
Death of the Fifth Sun, 113, 116,
  125
Dia de la Muerte (Day of the Dead),
  65
Dia de la Raza (Day of the Race),
  131
Díaz del Castillo, Bernal, 120-122,
  124

Dresden Codex, 63, *63*

El Castillo pyramid, *60-61*
El Tajin (city), 80, *81*, 82

Feathered Serpent, 34-35, 41-42, 50, 89, *112*, 113-114

glyphs, 47, 53-55
gods, 16-17, 19, 22, 23, 34, 38, 40, 49, 53-54, 62, 64-65, 71, 89, 92, 96-98, 108-109, *112*, 114-115, 120, 124-125
Great Pyramid at Cholula, 79
Guatemala, 31, 54-56, 65, 80, 102
Guelaguetza (festival), 75

Huitzilopochtli (god), 96-98, 108, 124

jaguars, 24, 26, 28, *30*, 30, 32-33
Lake Texcoco, 38, 98-100, 102
Landa, Diego de, 54
La Noche Triste (The Sad Night), 125, *126-127*
La Plaza de Tres Culturas (The Plaza of the Three Cultures), 129
La Venta, 28, *29*, 31-32
Legend of the Suns, 113
Long Count Calendar, 78
Los Voladores (The Flyers), 106, *107*

Maya Indians, 38, 77, 131
   and agriculture, 56, 58, 62
   and architecture, 56, 58
   and astronomy, 62-64
   calendar system, 52, 62
   climate, 55-56
   culture of, 54-56
   current society, 65
   decline of, 65
   legends and folklore, 53
   mathematical strengths, 55
   pyramids of, 55
   religious practices, 62, 64-65
   rituals, 59, 64-65
   social life and customs, 56, 58-59
   and sports, 63-64
   and writing, 53-54
Melgar, José Maria
Mesoamerica, 20, *20-21*, 22, 26-27, 34-35, 38, 42-43, 49, 54, 64, 70-71, 73, 79, 86, 92, 95, 99, 108, 115
Mestizos (La Raza), 131
Mexican flag, 98, *98*
Mexico City, 17, 19, 34, 37, 39, 86, 98, 102, 129-130
Mixtec people, 69, 72-73, 75, 79
Monte Albán (city), 22, *68-69*, *72-73*, 78, 89
   and agriculture, 71
   arts and crafts, 71, 73, 75
   construction of, 67
   culture of, 69-72
   geography of, 68
   history of, 68
   legacy of, 75
   as a military fortress, 69
   religious practices, 70-71, *74*
   social life and customs, 75
   and writing, 73
Montezuma II (emperor), 115-116, 120-125, *122-123*

Nahuatl language, 85-86, 93

Oaxaca, 68, 70-72, 75
Olmec Colossal Heads, 28, *29*
Olmec Indians, *24*, 78, 131
   accomplishments, 26
   arts and crafts, 28, 31

culture of, 25, 28, 30, 32
decline of, 32, 34-35
legacy, 35
military strengths, 34
and pyramids, 31-32
religious practices, 31-32, 34
social life and customs, 26, 34
stone heads, 26-28
and writing, 26-27

Palenque (city), 55
Paleo-Indians
and agriculture, 17-80
early settlement, 9-12
religious practices, 16-17, 22
rituals, 23
social life and customs, 15-16,
18-19, 22
Pecala (god), 71
Pre-Columbian Mexico, 78, 96, 131
Pyramid of the Feathered Serpent,
50
Pyramid of the Moon, 41-42,
44-45, 51
Pyramid of the Sun, 40-43, 41,
44-45, 51, 78
pyramids, 12, 26-27, 31-32, 34,
38-39, 39, 40, 41, 44-45, 46-47,
50-51, 55-56, 59, 60-61, 67,
79-80, 86, 99, 118, 124-125, 130

Quetzalcoatl (god), 89, 90-91, 92,
112, 113-114, 116, 120

San Lorenzo, 28, 32, 32-33
Spaniards, 41, 46, 54, 65, 71, 78,
82-83, 85, 88, 116, 116-117, 118,
120-125, 129, 131
Stela C. (tablet), 26-27
Stone of Tizoc, 103

stone sculptures, 32-33, 36, 66,
86-87, 128
Stone Warriors, 86

Temple of Quetzalcoatl, 90-91
Tenochtitlán, 76, 98, 99-100, 101,
102, 108, 115, 118, 120-122, 125,
130
Teotihuacán (city), 36, 40, 42, 78,
82-83, 86, 89, 90-91
and agriculture, 43
arts and crafts, 46-47, 49
climate, 49
demise of, 50-51
legacy of, 50-51
pyraminds of, 46
religious practices, 49
social life and customs, 43, 46-47
and sports, 49
and writing, 47
Tepantitla (mural), 47
The Discovery and Conquest
of Mexico, 121
The Drunkards (mural), 46
The Paradise of Tlaloc (mural),
48-49
Tikal (city), 55-56, 56-57, 64
Tizapan (place), 97-98
Tlaloc (god), 49, 94, 109
Toltec Indians, 38, 75, 78, 108, 114
and architecture, 86
arts and crafts, 89
culture of, 85, 87, 89
decline of, 92
as engineers, 88
legacy, 93
legends and folklore, 89, 92
military strengths, 87
and pyramids, 86
religious practices, 88-89, 92
rituals, 88

social life and customs, 92
Totonac Indians, 82
Tula (city), 86, *86-87*, 88, 92-93, 99
tzompantli shelves, 83, 83

Valley of Mexico, 19, 37-38, *76*, 83,
  86-87, 95, 97, 99, 102
Veracruz, 26-27, 80, 82, 118, 121

Yucatan, 56, 59, 87-88
Yucatan Peninsula, 12, 58

Zapotec Indians, *22*, 38, 69-73, 75, 77
Zócalo, 98, 130

PICTURE CREDITS